SOLDIER

A Member of the Perseus Books Group

SOLDIER

a poet's childhood

JUNE JORDAN

Published by Basic Civitas Books,

A Member of the Perseus Books Group

Book design by Victoria Kuskowski

FIRST EDITION

Library of Congress Cataloging-in-Publication Data

Jordan, June, 1936–

Soldier : a poet's childhood / June Jordan.

p. cm.

ISBN 0-465-03681-3

1. Jordan, June, 1936—Childhood and youth. 2. Poets, American—20th century—Family relationships. 3. Poets, American—20th century—Biography. 4. Jordan, June, 1936—Family. 5. Afro-American poets—Biography. 6. Afro-American families.

I. Title

PS3560.O73 Z47 2000

811'.54—dc21

[B] 00-023783

FOR MY FATHER

Honor thy father and thy mother.

EXODUS 20:12

And straightway the damsel arose, and walked;
for she was of the age of twelve years.

MARK 5:42

my gratitude

to my gracious and stalwart agent—and friend—Gloria Loomis, whose determination carried this story into the world

to my dauntless and brilliant critic and comrade, Sara Miles, for the strength of her cheering for the first full draft

to my insightful editor, Tim Bartlett, for the thoughtful depth and precision of his response

This story arrives, thanks to Laura Flanders
who believed in these words
and this poet.

This story stands, thanks to Peter Sellars
whose love upholds
the bird of dawn
that "singeth all night long."

PROLOGUE

I found the clothesline from a third-floor window of our brownstone more exciting than a rodeo.

I'd trail behind my father to the hardware store, and, while he and the other men lounging around the messy countertop talked baseball, New Deal politics, and the war, I'd finger a miscellany of nails and screws and washers and bolts, and I'd imagine a hundred different carpentry projects I could undertake or, in my full-blown fantasies, finish up.

Having chosen a solid pair of pulleys and more new white rope than I could carry, my father would stroll beside me, back to our job for the day.

He'd always say, "We gwine do *this*" or "We must to remember *that*," and I'd be so proud!

Our annual springtime collaboration was something I almost always forgot about entirely, until one Saturday morning, after an early breakfast, he'd hit the table with his fist and, knocking aside his chair, he'd issue one command to me: "Let's go!"

I was his helper, his sidekick: His son.

And this was a dangerous mission that only the two of us knew how to do.

He'd arrange things so I'd pass him a hammer or a screwdriver or a ruler the instant he called for it, while he bent and leaned and reached far beyond the boundary of the windowsill. I got it in my head that my speed guaranteed his safety. So I was fast, sometimes even mixing up the tool I should retrieve with the one he wanted next.

Sometimes the cold air flowing into my face would make me shiver and I'd want a handkerchief for my runny nose, but I would not budge from my assigned position and the dictates of my jittery alert.

In a slow moment I might notice how my father had dressed himself for the occasion: Khaki pants rumpling over old, slightly paint-speckled leather shoes, a belt aged to raw spots of color, and a clean but also slightly paint-speckled white tee shirt.

This was his Serious Business outfit.

And as my eyes might travel up to his well-muscled forearms and his compact, elegant hands, I'd be worrying, "What if he falls?"

I was too small. I was too weak.

He'd just fall, maybe the same way that I fell, again and again, in my recurring childhood dream: Falling and falling and falling and falling until I woke up.

It was terrifying to anticipate the possible smash termination to my irreversible, hurtling descent. A sudden racing of my heart convulsed my body and I felt a fatal inability to swallow or to scream aloud for help and so, as silent as a useless detail of an unknown and unknowable something else, I'd fall and fall and fall through the not usually sunlit atmosphere.

"What if he falls?"

As likely as not I'd be wearing a cowboy holster belt buckled around my hips; I'd be packing two toy pistols that clicked at the trigger and let you spin the chambers meant to restrain the killer bullets lodged there.

I knew I was not a cowboy. But I was practicing, a lot.

I already knew how to ride a horse. And if my long curls and butterfly barrettes didn't prevent my managing an animal that size, I couldn't see why there'd be a problem about, finally, escaping from my parents and heading out West to live on the range, "by my wits."

I was probably seven or eight years old when I began reading the Western tall tales written by Zane Grey. My father bought me two secondhand sets of books around this time: The novels of Sinclair Lewis (in blue hardback covers) and the complete works of Zane Grey (in orange hardback covers).

Lewis took me a while, and some threats and punishment, before I read anything of his all the way to the end.

But Zane Grey got me out on the desert or noticing cottonwood trees and building a fire, lonely, and blowing on boiling-hot black coffee in a tin cup hard to hold, and galloping mile after mile, hoping to stumble upon water, and, later, staring at stars, alone but tough and devoted to my horse, even though I'd be saddle-weary to the bone.

Whenever I let myself slide into any of his fabulous stories, Grey would carry me into new territory where I could hear a rattlesnake clear as a gunshot. And the start of this trip would take less than a page.

I adored the West. I had no idea where that might be, but I was pretty sure I'd have to skip out of my neighborhood for several days running before I'd be able to find it.

Meanwhile, I was comfortably packing two guns and watching my father risk the limits of a third-floor windowsill, and soon the two of us would bang down the stairs and noisily traverse the kitchen and then exit into the backyard, where we'd take on Phase Two: Installation of the Other Clothesline Pulley, twenty-five to thirty feet high on an otherwise ordinary telephone pole.

This was tricky.

My mother could see what was happening, now, and she'd be sure to object to my father's intention to climb that pole—and have me follow closely behind him.

This would mean an argument.

That would mean my mother losing to my father.

This would mean he'd go ahead as planned.

That would mean I'd duly imitate his every move, except that I'd remain, necessarily, closer to the ground.

This would mean my mother would disappear indoors and more or less hide inside her "little room," where she would probably begin to pray.

Once the emphatically outside pulley had been screwed

into place, and once the clothesline from the third-floor pulley draped around the interior wheel of its opposite, telephone pole, pulley, we were done!

Together we had measured and mastered requirements of height and depth and difficult connections, for all the world to see.

We were done!

And at this point we'd split apart.

I'd race up to that window and test the line, pushing it out and pulling it in, while my father, standing far below me, head up and smiling big, would bellow, "Push it out!" and "Pull it in!"

Then he'd laugh: "It works! It works!"

And I'd be grinning at him and just happy, until he'd tell me, "Close and lock the window!"

Back I'd race down the stairs and out to my father, who would hoist me to his chest and hug me hard and make a great commotion.

Then he'd place me on my feet and, bending down to peer into my eyes, he'd say:

"Tell you mother she have herself a clothesline now. And ask you mother why don' she wan' she try it out!"

So that would be my second dangerous mission for the day.

I would, of course, obey my father.

But before I'd leave him and the yard, and before I'd square my shoulders for the task ahead of me, I would gaze up and up along the gorgeous length of bright white line that lay across the open sky.

And I would conjure up the colors of the clothes that soon would fly and fill the air.

⁂

You never saw wild, or domesticated, horses on the Main Street, U.S.A., of Sinclair Lewis. Nobody acted like a cowboy. And picket fences and driveways in between neat patches of grass in the context of no shoot-outs and no canyons and no longing for a friendly wolf or a black-bottomed pot of beans and a familiar blanket-roll under your head while you slept, sometimes face to the rain, well, it didn't seem real to me.

Or interesting, in the least.

part one

HARLEM

I was born on the hottest day, in Harlem. A beastly heat set records while my mother labored more than twenty-five hours, alone, inside a shuttered hospital room.

No one gave her anesthesia or any other comfort.

The staff kept my father waiting beyond the closed door. And, stunned by her incessant weeping, her repetitive, weeping petitions to the Lord for some relief, he could scarcely decide whether to sit, to stand, or to smash up a chair, a pane of glass, a coffee cup.

My mother continued to moan. And she begged God to forgive her for these outbursts of ingratitude.

She was being blessed with a child. Months before, she had been visited in her sleep by angels who had told her that this firstborn would prove to be a great help to her people: Colored people. She was being blessed.

But she felt sundered by an agony that would subside only to return with a piercing intensity that lasted quite beyond her sensible endurance.

Her own sweat and bits of shit and blood drenched the sheets beneath her torment and she twisted and she toiled through arduous hours of her sacred tribulation, and she tried—she tried—to praise Jesus and His suffering as she suffered now, the curse of every woman.

This, then, was her cross to bear: This giving birth to me.

⁂

They were both West Indian immigrants. Both of them came to America from barefoot, peasant levels of poverty. But there the similarities disappeared.

My father quit after the first few months of grade school in Jamaica because, he said, the other children laughed at the rags he wore.

My mother completed the equivalent of high school and so, as my father reminded her, again and again, she knew how to read and write "long before" he got around to teaching himself those skills.

But my mother grew up in the dirt-floor cabin of a mountain village without electricity or running water. She would often whisper to me pictures of the frightening shadows of banana leaves below the changing message of the moon.

She came to this country because my grandmother, a domestic worker in New Jersey, finally sent for her.

My father came because his older brother, down in Panama, tried to take his teeth out with an ordinary pair of pliers.

Or: He came because he'd finished his stint as a British soldier who served in a cavalry regiment of Her Majesty's something or other in World War I.

It was hard to settle my father into a steady frame of reference.

He was a "race man," an admirer of Marcus Garvey, an enthusiast for theories about African origins of the human species, a zealous volunteer boxing instructor at the Harlem YMCA, devotedly literate in the available Negro poetry and political writings—and, also, he would angrily insist that he was *not* "black," *not* a "Negro."

Looking at him, you'd have to say that my father was extremely handsome, possibly white, and at least 50 percent Chinese.

Listening to him, you'd have to conclude that he was passionately confused and volatile.

Calling himself the Little Bull, my father was short, conspicuously fit, truculent, and generally (with women) flirtatious.

Believing that "idleness is the devil's plan," he stayed busy; reading through the night, his index finger tracking each syllable that he silently mouthed, or writing letters to government officials, or designing the next household or backyard project, or refining a schedule of forced enlightenment for me, his only child.

He was forever loquacious, argumentative, and visionary in his perspective.

And he was addicted to beauty, which is probably why he married my mother.

She had flawless brown skin and enormous dark brown

eyes. She was very beautiful. She was also very sad. But my father mistook her sadness for dignity, and he treasured her reserve, her hesitant pacing, her mysterious poise. He also savored the teasing of her artificial quiet, the fullness of her bosom, and her quivering lower lip. She walked that proud Jamaican walk, allowing for no haste, no misstep, no embarrassment of clumsy impulse.

He was a man's man. She was a man's woman, thrilled to be chosen by an unemployed, ambitious West Indian who would make her his wife: He would be the stubborn provider who would take proper care of her in this strange, fast-talking city.

And on the afternoon when he did at last get work, as an elevator operator, my father ran the whole length of Manhattan, uptown to their two cramped rooms, to shout, "A job! A job! I got a job!"

He intended to keep every single promise he made to her—and to himself.

All he wanted in exchange was her fidelity, her respect, a little loosening up on the affectionate side of things, and a son.

I loved orange juice. It seemed to me that orange juice and daylight fused in my mind as soon as I could focus. It was such a wonderful color! And you could see orange pulp particles moving inside that delicious liquid! A bottle or a glass of orange juice presented me with an aquarium that I could taste. And, oh! The pleasures of that color and that movement of that coloring on my tongue!

I could look and look at orange juice. I wanted and I hoped for and I never forgot about orange juice.

Milk was good for you.

I hated it.

But orange juice and the transparencies of glass and suffusing modulations of a day's light could and would excite me awake, my eyes wide open for more orange juice: More!

* * *

Half a year after I was born, it must have been Christmastime. The square rooms of our public-housing apartment felt crowded to me as many more visitors than usual came and went. A variety of unfamiliar voices boomed and lilted around the tree and my wicker bassinet.

My mother did not feel like starch or smell like food. I tried to reach for the tiny holiday rhinestones I saw sparkling around her neck and swaying from her ears. But she'd shake her head and tickle my stomach and singsong a nursery rhyme to distract me:

Hey diddle diddle
The cat and the fiddle
The cow jumped over the moon
The little dog laughed
To see such sport
And the dish ran away with the spoon

My mother had the habit of connecting a particular part of my body to every noun. For example, she'd say "Hey diddle diddle" and, at the second "diddle," she'd choose a spot—perhaps my cheek or the tip of my nose—and she'd press or pinch or kiss that chosen counterpart: "The *cat*" (scratching my elbow) "and the *fiddle*" (squeezing my thumb).

It's fair to say I could not help but fall in love with words. In this regard, my favorite rhyme was

This little pig went to market
This little pig stayed home
This little pig had roast beef
This little pig had none
This little pig cried wee, wee, wee!
All the way home

Quickly enough I learned I had five toes on each of my feet: My mother would wiggle them one at a time to identify each little pig, and, then, when she got to "all the way home," she'd bury her nose in my belly and giggle a soft sound that I liked to listen to.

Pretty soon my body had absorbed the language of all of the Mother Goose nursery rhymes, and my mother's dramatization of the rhythms of these words filled me with regular feelings of agreeable intoxication.

Even this:

There was an old woman who lived in a shoe
She had so many children she didn't know what to do
She gave them some broth without any bread
And whipped them all soundly and sent them to bed

Even that seemed wildly hilarious to me; I could hardly wait to hear it, again and again.

But except for Christmas, things stayed pretty quiet. My father talked to my mother. My mother talked to me.

* * *

And there was somebody else: Another child, my cousin, Valerie. She lived with us.

Until I got to be seven, my parents raised her as their own daughter.

She was four years older than I.

She looked like my mother: She resembled her so strikingly that passersby would often comment upon my mother's pretty little girl, and then, turning their attention to me, they'd ask, "Whose baby is this?"

⁂

Valerie was a musical prodigy and, while we were still living in Harlem, she actually held her debut piano recital at Little Carnegie Hall. With an astonishing memory, an uncanny mimic's gift, and huge almond eyes smothered by curly black eyelashes, she was, as everyone said, a remarkable, very pretty girl.

And shortly after I was born, Valerie was found trying to snuff me out. She was holding my baby pillow over my face and counting.

I don't think she was happy.

None of her childhood photographs shows her smiling.

⁂

If you happened upon my parents as they took their Sunday strut, pushing me forward in a top-security baby carriage, what you'd see, nailed as it were to this ponderous pram, were three initials: FDR. My father's attitude toward Franklin Delano Roosevelt verged on reverence. It was almost as though a member of our own family (presumably despite this and that hardship or temptation) had risen to power but then had never forgotten his lowly origins—which is to say, Roosevelt had not forgotten "the little man," Granville Ivanhoe Jordan.

Everything political filtered through my father on the most personal, intimately emotional terms. He would speak of this or that eminent politician as though no distance of any sort separated our family from this man's largesse or that other man's corruption.

Pictures of Roosevelt and the Queen of England and the Archbishop of the Diocese of Long Island hung on our parlor walls, not quite side by side.

But those visual reminders were superfluous, in fact. My father constantly invoked one or another world player in his daily conversation. And with ecstatic animation, he'd pursue his own game of "What you t'ink the Queen gwine do if—?!"

These were not moments of fanciful speculation, however. These were test questions intended to teach my mother, or later myself, about The Way Great People Go Through Life.

Locally, my father somehow got the mayor, Fiorello La Guardia, to hold me on his lap, and after that his ambitions for me bounded beyond the extraterrestrial.

He was not very predictable. Yes, he'd carefully chosen the Reverend Shelton Hale Bishop as my godfather. Father Bishop presided over Harlem's St. Phillip's Episcopal Church, an august Anglican edifice that, after my baptism, I was never taken to again. Apparently, attendance was not the point: It was official; I belonged to that fellowship. And, curiously, my godfather, as sophisticated as my father was naive, nevertheless chose to exert himself on my behalf all the way into my teens.

On the other hand, there was a practically self-proclaimed charlatan on the scene who dubbed himself Father Divine. My father patronized his rural outpost north of the city with unapologetic frequency. There his only child could see "real nature," drink milk from a cow she could touch, and marvel at steaming-hot hominy grits or crispy corn flakes with farm-fresh peaches sliced on top, their rough red hearts split into slippery bits and pieces of the entire tantalizing display.

These treats arrived at immaculate oilcloth-covered tabletops courtesy of nubile volunteer followers of Father Divine, adorned by names like Hope or Faith or Peace.

So evidently there were choices among churchly allegiances.

But inside the Jordan household nothing about religion was optional.

Along with Mother Goose nursery rhymes, my mother taught me prayers and most of the Old Testament. Her steady presentation of Little Bo Peep Who Lost Her Sheep differed in only one respect from her saturation recitation of the heroics of David against Goliath or Moses and the parting of the waters. When it came to God, there would be no tweaking of my toes. I was expected to learn about the Lord without rewards of related physical pleasure. So I did.

My mother held to her premonition about my usefulness to colored people. And shortly before my birth she shared her expectations with her church, the Universal Truth Center, which was housed above an incredibly wide and high flight of stairs on West 125th Street.

I don't think anybody minded about my mother's claims to an annunciation. It was just one more reason to praise God.

The minister, a woman everyone called Big Momma, affected a sequined turban and flowing sequined togas or gowns. She was the shepherd for three or four hundred colored women who idolized and utterly trusted her.

I suppose it was a Christian congregation. I know that Big Momma's creed centered on the powers of the Word. If you lost your wallet, you'd say, "There is no loss in the Divine Mind," and you'd believe that, and your wallet would turn up. If your neck was swollen with an elephantine thyroidal disorder, you'd say, "I am perfect in the Lord," and you'd believe it and that disorder would then shrink or disappear.

At the Universal Truth Center, the Word was nothing to play with.

And every week, my mother carried me there.

I got used to crowds of women surrounding me and prompting me "to say" anything, anything whatsoever.

And I can't imagine what my father was doing while all of this went on and on!

He must have been asleep.

But once he heard about my precocious singing at the church, my singing not just the melodies but the words of the hymns, he undertook to test and to observe me, more and more closely, for signs of intelligence.

⁂

This is when the fighting began.

I was not yet two years old.

Until then, I had assimilated everything from cereal and baby blankets to rhymes and stories and I had given nothing back, so to speak, besides a toothless gurgling or a watchful, fleeting look of concentration.

Now, my father decided, that was not enough. He wanted, he needed, to ascertain exactly what I was learning, and how. There would be no more mere listening to Sing a Song of Sixpence, a Pocketful of Rye / Four and Twenty Blackbirds Baked in a Pie!

It was my turn. He'd plod through a rhyme out loud, and then I'd be tested: Could I recite that myself?

I could.

Well then, how much was four and twenty?

Of course, even the question was meaningless to me.

No matter! Clearly I must learn to count. I must pay attention to the four and twenty pale green peas he now rolled across the floor.

He would teach me about numbers.

And further, to that end, he purchased a miniature abacus with green and blue and yellow wooden beads that easily flew back and forth on straight, colorless rods.

I was given an illustrated hardcover Mother Goose and, alternating with my mother, he read to me the rhymes I had already memorized.

Next he'd encourage me to open my large new Mother Goose and "find," for example, Jack and Jill Went Up the Hill.

Done?

Okay: Read it to him—backward.

As he assumed control, he advised my mother that she, in effect, had been dismissed.

He knew what had to be done.

He'd do it.

I'd do it.

She'd see, very soon, that his decision was the right decision.

They argued about who was more likely to "spoil" or "ruin" me.

My father's voice got loud.

My mother didn't say much, but she never said, "All right."

She was fighting.

They were fighting.

They were fighting with each other.

I had become the difference between them.

⁂

Thanks to his energetic outreach and persistent inquiries, my father moved us into the Harlem River public housing projects only days after city officials cut the inaugural ribbon.

I was still a baby.

It was going to seem like paradise to me. All of the low-rise red brick buildings matched rather nicely, and sapling maple trees asserted themselves in the freshly planted dirt that bordered pedestrian paths. To the west, space enough for four lanes of traffic created a very generous conduit for natural light. To the east, a gigantic sloping lawn drew you down to the river where tugboats and occasional cargo freighters floated by.

That man-made valley of light to one side and the slow flowing of the river on the other never failed to salvage a morning or an afternoon from any sense of confinement or doom.

Whenever I was taken outside I felt like singing and, very often, I did just that. I sang out loud:

Jesus loves me
This I know
For the Bible
Tells me so
Little ones to Him belong
They are weak but He is strong!
Yes . . .

⁂

My mother's wedding picture portrays a young woman standing in white satin and lace. It is as though this is the snapshot of a statue no one can identify. She will not move. She does not breathe. She stands attuned to the timing of an event she can neither comprehend nor compromise. The slant of her beautiful head mystifies the camera, and her lowered eyes appear to pity the bridal train of languid lace that spills past her feet, on the floor.

This young woman is no one I ever knew.

⁂

I was two. People asked me how old I was so often that I got used to thinking, "I am two." My parents talked about me that way.

They'd say, "She's two."

I thought two was who I was.

Maybe I should have been born a boy. I think I dumbfounded my father. Whatever his plans and his hopes for me, he must have noticed now and again that I, his only child, was in fact a little girl modeling pastel sunbonnets color-coordinated with puffy-sleeved dresses that had to accommodate just-in-case cotton handkerchiefs pinned to them.

I'm not sure.

Regardless of any particulars about me, he was convinced that a "Negro" parent had to produce a child who could become a virtual whiteman and therefore possess dignity and power.

Probably it seemed easier to change me than to change the meaning and complexion of power.

At any rate, he determined he'd transform me, his daughter, into something better, something more likely to succeed.

He taught me everything from the perspective of a recruiting warrior. There was a war on against colored people, against poor people. I had to become a soldier who would rise through the ranks and emerge a commander of men rather than an infantry pawn.

I would become that sturdy, brilliant soldier, or he would, well, beat me to death.

⁂

One morning when I was about two and a half years old, my father transported me downtown, away from my mother. Everybody looked large to me, and white. We went inside the Ethical Culture School and some lady kept smiling at me but I didn't know why so I watched her without saying anything and I stayed inside my father's arms until they put me in a room with chickens: Feathery yellow chickens!

I had never seen chickens before and there was a funny smell to them and they zigzagged or skittered about and I enjoyed the whole thing.

I'm not sure what happened there, but I guess it was a test situation of some sort. And my test score and the teachers who assessed me there evidently persuaded my father that he had a genius—or a monster—on his hands. And from that downtown trip forward, anything like a regular childhood lay entirely behind me.

Now, whenever possible, my father would carry, prod, or toddle me across the Harlem River Bridge, for two reasons: To drill me in techniques of observation and to increase my breathing stamina.

I'd be instructed to hold my breath as long as I could while noticing how many tugboats of what color passed below us, or how many people of what kind or age had passed us by.

He called this "military reconnaissance training" and he explained to me that one could never get too good at this sort of exercise: It might save your life.

I didn't like all the questions all of the time, but I liked it when he held my hand.

⁂

As usual, my father had been holding my hand when, unexpectedly, he swung me into the air by my arm, at the same time commanding me to stop that swinging of my body any way I could. But I couldn't stop it. And he lost my hand and I went flying headfirst into the outside corner of a stone building. This accident split my forehead and there was a great deal of blood and I could see and I could hear my father crying and yelling for help.

I still have that scar.

⁂

When he went away to work, when my father left my mother and me alone, I was allowed to indulge my more solitary inclinations.

My mother would position a zinc tub on the sloping lawn behind our apartment. She'd attach a toy laundry wringer, fill that tub halfway with water, and bring me a pile of doll's clothing to wash and wring dry. This was bliss.

She'd leave me there.

My father would not suddenly appear and beat or threaten me with "the strap."

Nobody bothered me. I could splash and play, bemused by the creamy iridescence of soap-flake spray. I could contemplate the watery reflections of so many no-longer-definite things: My face or the drastic attenuation of an overhead branch. And meanwhile I was washing my clothes!

I never wearied of this make-believe.

And it was only partly not true.

Yes, the clothes were not dirty, for starters, and, yes, I never got around to rinsing out the soap, but other than that I was really washing clothes, and when I lifted my eyes from the tub, or if I looked beyond the handle of the wringer, I could always see the Harlem River, always bright and always sliding along.

Otherwise, she'd bring out a miniature tin tea set, complete with teapot, cups, and saucers, and I'd settle one or two dolls across from me and, since I'd never seen any grown-ups "take tea," there was nothing I had to remember or emulate.

I'd sit there and wait for "The Tea" to happen.

And I'd continue to sit and to wait, with my dolls.

And I liked this peculiar ritual a lot.

But mostly, with or without my father in the house, I spent my time reading. And mostly, I did not understand what I could nevertheless decipher and pronounce correctly.

Like the story of the boy who was eating a doughnut and his sister begged him for a bite and he said, "I'll save you the hole," and she anxiously watched while he continued to devour the doughnut and, when he had finished, she cried, "Oh! But you promised me the hole!," and he laughed at his sister and told her not to cry because he had kept his word: The hole was nothing but air and she had air around her, didn't she?

I didn't understand that joke.

But my parents had chosen *The Ugly Duckling* as my first storybook.

From front to back, that softcover book contained a single story with black-and-white illustrations. And I thought, I was certain, that I understood what I was reading, and it shocked me.

What was *ugly*? It seemed to mean the wrong family and no friends and other ducks refusing to play with you and making fun of however you didn't look exactly like them.

And I had never heard about *ugly* before. And *ugly* frightened me. I was afraid and then I became positive that I might be *ugly*.

Why did the Ugly Duckling lose its mother?
How could a duck turn into a swan?
Why would that be a happy ending for a duck?
The Ugly Duckling was depicted as a black baby duck.
The swan was white.
How did the black baby duck turn white?
Why was that a happy ending?

I thought I understood that story,
and I didn't believe it,
and I kept reading it to myself,
over and over.

⁂

I never wanted and I never got a Shirley Temple doll.

⁂

Patricia Cantwell was my best friend. We shared a tricycle, and the same nursery-school teacher, and apples, and large jars of white poster paste, and crockery pots of red and blue paint, and I thought she was perfect because we were identical in height and because her mother wore lipstick and long long fingernails with red nail polish and, once, her mother made lunch for both of us, and I guess she must have sliced and sautéed mushrooms for us to eat, but I didn't know what mushrooms were and so I decided mushrooms must be some kind of half-alive animal or maybe warmed up, flattened–out worms, and because she served them with her long long fingernails flickering obvious, I thought they must be also very glamorous, grown-up creatures, besides, but I didn't know the word *mushrooms,* so I couldn't ask or tell anybody about this unforgettable secret that, year after year, I kept hoping to be surprised by, one more time.

⁂

At some point I vaguely concluded that I would be lucky if I could look like five-year-old Dolores Edwards, who lived on the first floor, when I grew up. Dolores had dimples on both sides of her mouth.

⁂

Hitler, Charlie Chaplin, and my father were men who sported a mustache. Hitler was a bad man. Charlie Chaplin was a funny man. And my father was my father.

There was a famous man who gave up "the throne" for "the love of a woman." And at the Palace of Father Divine you could buy delicious chicken dinners for fifteen cents a plate.

In our house, my mother became a subscriber to *The Daily*

Word, which paired each day to a Biblical verse. And for me she subscribed to *Wee Wisdom,* which wallowed in abstract graphic designs and moral admonitions reinforced by didactic crossword puzzles.

I loved *Wee Wisdom* because it was mine and because everything in it was orange.

* * *

I didn't know it but my father was preparing to move us out of Harlem. Brooklyn, he said, was a better place for a man to raise a family. White people lived in Brooklyn.

Everything would be better for us.

"Me no gwine to stay in a ghetto, you see?!" And he'd conjure up cozy private homes and clean streets and a backyard "so the children, dem, can play."

And I wondered why we needed to move anywhere, because I was very happy.

* * *

I guess I had decided that physical was the way to go in moments of unusual stress, and so when my cousin, Valerie, was being picked on and smacked about and kicked by another girl one afternoon, I broke a Coke bottle on the pavement and went after that girl, managing to cut what I could easily reach. So I slashed her leg. And I broke up that fight. And I also acquired my Harlem reputation as "one crazy little girl."

I think my father somehow got into trouble about that, but he found the entire incident hilarious and I noticed that he seemed to be very proud of me.

I must have been about four years old.

Valerie was, of course, bigger and taller than I. And from my point of view, we were still not close—or, not especially. But she was part of my family and that girl was beating the daylight out of her. So I did what I thought I should do.

My mother absolutely disagreed. She insisted that (little) girls (meaning, specifically, me, her daughter) "do not fight."

My father said that, generally speaking, one should not hit a girl under any circumstances. By "one," my father meant *a boy* or *a man*.

I got the message that a real man would never strike a woman or a girl. But this was rather confusing to me because my father regularly "struck" me, for example, whenever he felt I had violated any of his precepts or disrespected any of his multiple assignments.

Nevertheless, I was clear about one thing: A really excellent way to stop somebody from hitting you is to hit them back.

One morning the split between religious and regular words disappeared.

My mother had been reading aloud the Scripture for the day. Now she came to something about "Verily the Lord saith" and I started to giggle and laugh. I begged her to say it again, and as soon as she reiterated "Verily," I collapsed into a second giggling fit.

I knew the song "Merrily we roll along, roll along, roll along"—and that was just something you could sing for fun. But "Verily" and "Merrily" sounded almost the same to me, and I was so excited about that!

I marched around, shouting, "Merrily and Verily! Merrily and Verily!" for quite a while until Valerie, with a disgusted grimace, told me to knock it off.

* * *

I wonder how the Little Bull, my father, got the money and a mortgage to buy a house in Brooklyn.

* * *

Maybe we were going there to say good-bye. My mother never explained that part of the trip, but she bundled me into my Sunday chocolate-colored snowsuit, and I wore a favorite dress underneath: The top of it crinkled up in smocking stitches, and you could see almost invisible birds in flight, if you looked carefully. And I looked.

At any rate, we were taking a daylong trip to the house of Big Momma, who lived in Elizabeth, New Jersey. I was to be on my "company" behavior, and my mother washed and combed and brushed and oiled and braided my hair until my scalp felt sore.

I could tell she was excited and nervous, and no amount of humming to herself could fool me.

This appeared to be an honor, this invitation to visit our big lady minister. It had never happened before.

My father was staying behind at home. He would take care of himself and Valerie until we got back.

I began to feel puzzlement and something like dread.

It was a long journey. We rode the subway and then we walked and then we boarded a railroad train with a conductor in a black uniform and a cap, just like the train conductors in my storybooks.

It was a long journey. I was half asleep when my mother roused me awake, and I could hear the conductor calling out "Eee-lizzz-ah-beth!"

On the platform, there was Big Momma, standing alert, with a welcoming smile, and another woman stood beside her, and both of them looked like white people to me. This was pretty surprising. So I doublechecked Big Momma for her smile, because she didn't look like Big Momma anymore to me. I didn't know a lot of white people and I wasn't sure about whatever I didn't know and, besides, once my mother and I got on a bus and I said hello to the white bus driver and he didn't say hello to me and he didn't smile at me or anything and I got upset about this and made quite a fuss.

And to calm me down, I suppose, my mother told me that "some people are born that way; some people are born not able to smile even if they want to." I think she hoped I'd feel sorry for the bus driver, and I did, a little bit, but mostly he scared me, and I could see that he was a white man and I did think maybe that was the problem.

And on another occasion my father and I were walking down Seventh Avenue when we came upon a white man who was wearing a policeman's uniform and a policeman's badge and a policeman's gun, and he was also a fat man, so I rushed up to him and poked him in the stomach as hard as I could and I said, "Get away from me, fat man!," and my father was frightened out of his wits and I couldn't decide if that was because the man was fat, or because the man was a police officer, or because he was white. But whatever the reason, I always hated policemen after that.

I didn't like seeing my father afraid of anything or anybody.

I already viewed fat people with something akin to contempt. This was a color-blind prejudice incubated by my father's maniacal dedication to soldierly fitness for me. Just about as soon as I could stand without immediately falling down, my father had launched his lifelong battle against what would become of me if I forgot to hold my head up, push back my shoulders, suck in my gut, and "Stride straight ahead!"

On the other hand, there was the friendly fat mayor, Fiorello La Guardia, and my nursery-school teacher. They were white people, too.

And now, minus her turban and toga, there was Big Momma looking white herself. Her commonplace outfit made me uncomfortable. Was she still Big Momma?

Big Momma had parked her car some distance from the train station, and as we moved away from the platform I slowed myself down and fell behind, studying the ground under my feet and musing on the chunks of coal I'd seen beneath the railroad ties. I wanted to get back on the train.

But we drove to Big Momma's house. It was large from the outside, and dull and cluttered and shadowy inside. She had no children. She had no husband. It was very quiet.

My mother and Big Momma murmured and whispered in an awkward zigzag. The other woman appeared and invited everyone "for tea."

I was thrilled, upright in my chair: A "tea," at last!

And, just as I'd placed cups and saucers in front of myself

and my dolls, the other woman in Big Momma's house prepared the same for us.

The only differences were teaspoons and a sugar bowl and a pitcher for cream. (The creamer did not have a teaspoon in it.)

In the meantime, my mother sat chatting about "china" and the "aroma" of the tea.

Apparently gratified, Big Momma leaned forward and, smiling without reservation, she exclaimed, "Oh! But you must call me Fergie!"

My mother repeated the new word: "Fergie?"

"Well, yes!" Big Momma reassured her. "That's, actually, that's my name!"

And she paused to enjoy the effect of this sudden information.

But my mother had nothing to say.

I, on the other hand, was almost beside myself: Fergie!? Big Momma was Fergie?!

But to my infinite disappointment, there was no more talk about names or about tea. My mother pretended she hadn't heard anything special.

So things got worse, and then they got worse.

I consumed a sickening number of peppermint candies and wondered what would happen next.

We had been expected to stay for supper, but my mother

asked Big Momma to excuse us; she said she was not feeling well, and we would therefore have to leave.

I was so glad! I loved my mother! She was getting us out of there!

More quickly than ever, my mother bundled me back into my snowsuit and fastened a rather bright scarf around my neck. As we drove back to the train station, Big Momma said it was a shame that we hadn't even prayed together, but I felt no regret. I needed to make up my mind about Big Momma and who she really was. And no matter what, I would never again believe words coming out of her mouth.

At the Universal Truth Center she had not been telling us the truth. She had told us a lie about her name. And I suspected that my mother was not feeling well because Big Momma was actually not Big Anything, as far as she could see.

It was so cold on the railway platform. It was so cold and so dark that I pressed my head against my mother's overcoat until, finally, she put her arm around me.

That helped, but not much.

We were waiting for the train. We shifted from one frost-bitten foot to the other, waiting in the icy air. We stood there so long that all I wanted was to stop struggling not to freeze.

Then we heard a moaning in the dark. And, as startling as

a transitory signal from a hidden fire, the huge eye of a locomotive eased its promise into the night and, growing large, grew larger, and everything around me shook and shuddered as that engine pulled alongside the platform, lurching, awful, to a halt.

I had never felt worshipful before that. But there was no arguing with the enormity of that black locomotive traveling, hell's bells, on two million steel wheels.

I could scarcely believe the beauty of that solitary beam of light as it engorged itself inside my eyes.

I completely forgot about Big Momma as my mother settled us on a fuzzy double seat of that long-awaited train. And presently she held me close. And I soon fell asleep, all the long way home.

part two

BROOKLYN

Like a growling beast, the roll-away mahogany doors rumble open, and the light snaps on and a fist smashes into the side of my head and I am screaming awake: "Daddy! What did I do?!"

And now he lays on a belt, slapping the leather and the buckle hard against the blankets or my arm exposed by short-sleeve teddy-bear pyjamas.

And I am trying to cover my face and he tears away the blankets and I can barely recognize this man, my father.

It is 2 or 3 A.M. He has just come home. He has finished the night shift at the post office.

He's tired.

He's furious:

"You damn black devil child!"

And with every word another blow bludgeons my body or my head again.

I am silent and I concentrate on blocking the blows as they fall.

Or I begin to answer back: "Stop!"

Or: "Don't hit me! Please, Daddy! Please don't hit me!"

And his beating me continues until he's spent and his fury subsides. Then he snaps off the light with a warning:

"Me gwine talk s'more tomorrow."

And I hear him rumble shut those doors, those cursed phony walls that never hold together to protect me, and I guess I am supposed to settle myself back to sleep.

But in the darkness I am listening to his footsteps: Is he, in fact, going away or coming back?

I crouch there, in that lonely aftermath, listening until there is no sound left in the whole house besides my own furtive breath.

⁂

My father hurt me but I never knew why.

⁂

I was five years old and I do not remember how we moved away from Harlem.

⁂

Brooklyn was supposed to be different, and it was. It was like this great big painting of a new life that never fit inside its frame.

All the toil and the shenanigans and fantasy and trust that went into my father's purchase of the deed to our house suddenly lay behind him: A poor man's miscellany of small spurts and grandiose seizures that nearly overwhelmed his sense of direction.

And what, now, would lend him support? Now, when he craved congratulations and other kinds of confirmation that the property to which he held the title in his hand and in his name—that this, that *his* property was not a monument to mock him: A tombstone testimonial to a terrible mistake.

It had been so hard to come by!

Surely that was evidence of its absolute value.

And was there another way a man should be a man and keep a wife and "raise him up a family"?

My mother seethed with disappointment and chagrin. What kind of people could have lived "like this"?

She fumed about the former occupants of our new home. They had been dirty people. They had been filthy people. They had been Germans. And Germans were white: They had been white people:

"Why did you father have to drag us out to nowhere anybody can see and set us down in what the white people them thrown out?!"

Yanking me along beside her, my mother inspected the three-story brownstone, pointing to discolored, chipped-away linoleum, warped or rotted wood joints, water-stained ceilings, and the darkness of the hallways and the rooms. She shook her head. She muttered to herself. She took me up and down and up the two flights of stairs, slower each time, because in the whole house there was not a single closet anywhere and because in the whole house there was not one bathroom.

Or, as she reiterated:

"Over here is a toilet. Over there is a sink with a cold running water. And where is the bathroom?"

❧ ❧ ❧

I didn't like the house too much. I couldn't find anywhere warm to stand or sit. Well, there was one place, but that was supposed to be off-limits.

And how I loved that forbidden, secret zone. I would sneak into it, the cellar, almost tiptoe down a short precarious slant of steps so old you couldn't grasp what passed for a wooden railing without coming away with flakes of paint, of splinters, in your hand. But once you reached cracked concrete at the base of everything, cobweb gobs stretched overhead near a roaring furnace and a huge coal bin that I eagerly climbed into and scrambled across and hid inside. I liked to pretend that I was resting on a mountaintop nobody else could see.

And then there was the coal itself: I would snuggle all over it, feeling myself surrounded by small rocks of immense mystery and the most gorgeous coloring.

Besides the cellar, I liked the tall narrow windows and the stained-glass skylights and also the roof, which, consistent with my mother's evaluation of our new abode, needed immediate, extensive, expensive, and recurring repair.

But it was our roof. And my father would take me there

and teach me how to tread lightly in order not to worsen its shattering-crust surface. Then he'd cajole or dare me to approach the edge of it: That way I'd have "the best view" and, also, I'd get over any fears I might have of (dangerous) heights.

It was surprising to see things below me and far away. I tried to appreciate that shocking perspective. But the connection between distance and what you could see confounded me. What did it mean to behold everybody's backyard only when I stood quite beyond and above each one of them, including my own?

I had trouble with the challenge of the limits of the roof.

I never really enjoyed the game of getting closer and closer to the end of anything under my feet.

But I never let on that I was terrified to the pit of my stomach. Just as I never once cried or allowed tears to spill from my eyes when my father attacked me: Never.

I think (or I thought) that, partly, that was why my father became so violent and apparently out of control: I never cried. I refused to. And instead I concentrated on things like his position or my position or the proximity of this or that possible escape.

He had taught me well.

I had to practice a complicated litany of manly virtues and combat skills.

You never took your eyes off the eyes of your opponent.

You never showed any weakness or admitted to any pain.

You watched for every opening to strike or to defend yourself.

In a situation of unequal strength or weight or height, everything was "fair."

The factor of surprise was always a first-choice weapon.

And fearlessness, or the appearance of no fear, was key to psychological poise and resistance.

But these lessons did not happen in a rhetorical realm.

By the time I was five years old, my father had begun regular assault exercises: He'd constantly test me by coming up from behind and wrapping an arm around my throat and telling me to "make me let you go." Or I'd be walking into the kitchen and he'd say something in a soft voice that I couldn't hear, exactly, and as I got nearer to him he'd throw a surprise left-and-right-hook combination of punches I was expected to block.

The point was to stay on the alert.

The point was not to be beaten.

And so my father also taught me how to box: Footwork, and bobbing and weaving my head, and never to straighten out on a punch but instead to keep my body's weight loading into the force of my fist.

All of this made my mother crazy.

She tried to budge my father out of these pugilistic ambitions for me by dismissing our various combat drills as just "a foolishness."

But he, my father, was not to be deterred.

And he taught me well.

I learned to pump myself past dread and, if necessary, even to relish the need to fight. And although I didn't think of it that way, it was nevertheless true that I was learning, most specifically, to fight my father.

* * *

Inside the new house there was tumult and hammering and scattered boxes and mops and brooms and so much confusion! But I remember something large and heavy that my parents called a snake plant and I watched it for quite a while. But nothing about it moved or turned. And I remember thick winter drapes that did resemble snakeskin or crocodiles or silvery and slithery folds of material hanging over translucent white curtains that held the most wonderful hot smell and the most wonderful billows of visible dust particles. And sunlight used to wriggle or stream or dart through those curtains and splash or streak all over the floors.

* * *

In the Harlem River Housing Projects we had lived in a coherent, planned community with look-alike buildings and look-alike Black American and West Indian families bustling among look-alike pedestrian pathways that curved among look-alike patterns of planted grass and trees.

Our apartments were uniformly neat and modern, with solid white walls and fully equipped kitchens, with closets and shelves and cupboards, with hot and cold running water and radiator heat that you simply turned on and off.

Eligibility criteria stipulated an income not to exceed working-class or working-poor wages and, evidently, urgency based upon race.

In New York City there were very few places anybody not "white" could live. Landlords and realtors openly and legally discriminated against "colored" applicants.

So public housing was more than a godsend. It was actually a necessity and safe harbor for Black families.

And while we lived within the benign design of that friendly, familiar environment, I do not recall any tension about money or any qualms about our quality of life. Like everyone around us, we were striving hard, spit-and-polish clean, and therefore bound to "better ourselves."

Days went by uneventfully and, I thought, happily.

My father would hit or shake me hard or squeeze my upper arm until it ached, but he did not beat me, on and on and on, until after we left Harlem.

I progressed from nursery rhymes and *The Ugly Duckling* to Donald Duck and *Rebecca of Sunnybrook Farm*, which reduced me to tears of laughter because Rebecca herself had laughed and laughed at something a young man visiting her had happened to say, until she rolled off the porch of her parents' house and landed on top of a rosebush, still laughing.

Compulsory reading assignments and next-day examinations by my father did not become an incessant, peculiar component of my weekly routine until after we left Harlem.

And I never heard the word *sacrifice* until we moved to Brooklyn.

Suddenly I had to listen to my mother and my father talking about sacrifice, day in and day out. I was told to remember sacrifice or to be worthy of sacrifice or to be grateful for sacrifice.

And as far as I could see, sacrifice was not a good idea. It never made anybody laugh. It would never bedevil a hard-boiled egg.

I turned completely against sacrifice. But nobody asked me.

And the worst part of sacrifice was that it was supposed to be happening for my sake: My "future."

But really, what I could tell for sure about sacrifice was that Brooklyn was where it began and that sacrifice sent my father away to work through the night and sacrifice took my mother away to work part of every night and so sacrifice left me alone a lot of the time when it was dark inside the house and out.

I hated sacrifice.

⁂

Brooklyn increased our living space 300 percent, but once we got there everything tightened up and felt crowded and jumpy and sounded like an argument to me but, for sure, it was seldom boring at 681 Hancock Street.

⁂

I cannot imagine how my father managed the bunches of THINGS TO DO that kept him whirling around, stubborn and frequently enthusiastic.

First of all, he had to create A BATHROOM for my mother or she was never going to stop fussing about it.

So he decided to convert a fraction of the kitchen into the most fabulous bathroom he could dream up and build. There would even be fluorescent lights and silver swans on pink and ivory wallpaper that, somehow, he found time to buy. There was going to be an ivory-colored toilet and sink, and a medicine cabinet and a mirror, and a bathtub and shower and hand-laid multicolored floor tiles that he, my father, was going to install, piece by little piece.

All of this meant major construction that seemed scheduled never to end. There was a new dividing wall that my father decided should curve slightly outward from its middle point. But this plan swamped him in byzantine calculations that forced him to measure and remeasure I don't know how many times until he figured out appropriate techniques to accomplish his brainstorm.

And then he decided to reserve the entire top eighteen inches of that wall for beveled glass that would, he explained to me, admit natural light flowing from the kitchen and therefore "save on the electricity bill!"

This design decision further complicated the bathroom saga; and my mother, waiting, as she said, for just "a normal bathroom," grew increasingly hostile to the elaborate messy project that altogether wrecked her tidy kitchen arrangements.

Could he never have done with it?

But my father wanted the bathroom to finish up so pretty and so unusual that she'd know for certain that he had meant the new house as a tribute and a gift to her: Not some awful, impractical joke.

I didn't care about any of this. I liked the smell of wet cement and I liked the gleam of the wires and the shine of the pipes that appeared and disappeared. And since I didn't like food or eating anyway, I was happy that it was difficult to find or cook or concentrate on cereal or liver or spinach or eggs or anything, really, besides ice cream or canned peaches and a slice of pound cake and a glass of milk!

Regardless, my place was at the kitchen table. I would sit there and study or read, trying to appear impervious to the grown-up drama around me. I had to. Between school and my father, I was forever on assignment. And there was nowhere else, no flat surface, for me to write or rest a book upon.

Writing was difficult for me. My penmanship was bad. I copied the letters of the alphabet over and over, slowly and fast, but they never looked right. And whenever I erased a letter you could always tell.

It was interesting to try to match up letters from the alphabet with a word in my head. But I was baffled about *b–a–l–l* never looking like what it was supposed to mean no matter how carefully I printed or placed the letters, one after the other.

Meanwhile, my cousin, Valerie, was playing the piano and her fingers did seem to fly among the keys and, for the most part, she sounded right. I liked to hear her play the piano. I liked to watch her reading the music with her eyes and using her fingers to express what she saw in her notes.

So I felt inspired.

I thought that maybe if I paid more attention to the sound of words I would be able to write better. And I tried to listen more and more closely to the syllables and the vowels and everything I could possibly notice about words.

I began to think about words as a kind of music.

And this was very fortunate for me, because my father had begun to require me to read and attest to things I could not understand. But because the music, for example, of Edgar Allan Poe's poetry or Paul Laurence Dunbar's poetry or Shakespeare's sonnets was so obvious, I was able, pretty easily, to recite passages from memory, on demand—and this tended to placate, if not entirely satisfy, my father. But I was performing, strictly, in fact, by ear.

I never quite understood the new house. But my first boyfriend lived directly across the street. His name was Carlyle. He was blond and blue-eyed, with curly hair and a rather deep voice for a six-year-old, and, outside of a book, I had never seen such a cute boy before.

As soon as it seemed polite to do so, I asked him if he was a Negro. When he said yes, I said I was a Negro, too, and I remember feeling excited by how much we, right away, had in common.

I loved his name. It was so beautiful that I almost never said it out loud. I felt too shy. I felt that if that name came out of my mouth, its beauty alone would reveal something too embarrassing to say.

But Carlyle was not shy. He was definite. He told me I was

his girlfriend and that when we grew up we would get married and that if he ever caught me with another boy he'd kill me.

He spoke in short, gruff sentences, but his dimples showed anyway, and I was glad so much about my life had been settled so quickly.

I met and basically became committed to Carlyle during the second week of our new life in Brooklyn.

He was a little bit bigger and a little bit older than I, and he was a boy, so we didn't really play together very much, but he stood around a lot, and I liked looking at him, and there was a strong, bony cut to his chin and his shoulders, and best of all, there was something about his voice that thrilled me.

* * *

I didn't know where Valerie slept, or if she slept at all.

There was one large bedroom with a large bed in it and various crocheted coverings and pillows and white sheets, but I never saw my parents in that bed or any other.

I don't know if they slept anywhere in the house.

Big bureaus guarded the bed, and some of the drawers held more sheets or stacks of my father's shirts, but I am certain I never saw either of my parents lying down in a bed.

But still, there was that bedroom, the only bedroom of the house, really, and one of its walls was fake: Two floor-to-ceiling mahogany doors rolled back and forth on tracks, and on the other side of that fake wall was supposed to be my room.

It was extremely narrow, but there was a long window at one end and a regular door that never opened or closed at the other. Then there was a water closet with an ancient sink inside and nothing else. And then there was a single bed, where I slept, and next to that a small bookcase packed with Zane Grey Westerns and the complete works of Sinclair Lewis.

Above my bed was an overhead light. And on the walls, to my exasperated disbelief, there was light green wallpaper criss-crossed by beribboned bouquets of red roses, and I could never persuade my father to change it to white walls with a navy blue ceiling, just as I could never influence my father about the color of my beloved wooden wagon, which he painted and repainted lime green inside and raspberry red around its perimeter.

But he kept whirling around until the new house began to look and smell new and fresh, and after he'd lay down new linoleum in the hallway or on the stairs, my father would wax and polish it on his knees, and he'd be whistling and sweating and proud, and because the wanting condition of the house provoked so much upheaval and replacement and renovation I think my mother gave up on housekeeping pretty much altogether, just as she gave up on raising me, except for teaching me to pray and dressing me up and washing and combing my hair.

I was five and a half years old.

* * *

Let me be more precise. My mother shopped for the groceries.

Milk

Bread

Meat

That was the list. And she composed it, week after week, with the same obvious concentration. I watched. I waited. Her pencil poised above the back of a used envelope. She seemed to be listening for something. A hint, or a different idea. And then, one at a time, those words would emerge again: *Milk. Bread. Meat.*

But in fact the grocery cart would fill up with crackers and cake and cookies and a pink-and-blue box of "luncheon napkins" and hot sauce and celery and bacon and waxed paper and a few other things she might stare at, not blinking, for quite a while.

Her hands looked poor to me: Meager and naked and closed around that list, or seven or eight dollar bills, or a can of tomato soup, or a jar of peanut butter.

And when we got home I'd bolt about, putting things away, but my mother would just sit there, often in her overcoat, apparently confused or disappointed by the outcome of our expedition.

My mother also washed the laundry. She sorted, and then she placed the clothes and the socks and the sheets and the towels in crazy pileups on the kitchen floor. Next she attached a large wringer contraption onto one side of the double kitchen sink and set out a gigantic zinc tub beside the wash.

Now her prodigious work began: Rubbing each item hard across a scrubboard sloping into the soapy water and maneuvering the faucet into a running rinse position, and then angling whatever it might be in between the rubber cylinders that squeezed it free from dripping water, and at last dropping the clean wet socks or shirt into the tub.

I could smell the soap and the bleach. My mother's fingers grew purple and swollen, almost bursting their water-tortured skin. And she'd keep at it, this hard work, silently, while the radio broadcast World News and Interviews or Amos and Andy or Cream of Wheat Is So Good to Eat That I Eat It Every Day. And I wished she'd say anything at all besides, very infrequently, when it was really, really hot, asking me to wipe away the sweat from her brow, "with a rag."

Occasionally my grandmother came to visit and she'd help my mother with the laundry. They'd stand at diagonal corners and fold sheets as though they were dancing toward each other, and I sat at the table watching them laugh about secret things and never stopping to rest, and if I ever tried to help they'd laugh some more and tell me, "Put your nose back in a book!"

So I never got to try.

⁂

I was never allowed to do anything like housework. I never washed dishes or set the table or cooked or made my bed or, for that matter, combed my own hair.

My father assumed all of the chores of the regular cleaning and all of the major cooking, especially Jamaican rice and peas, which he prepared in weekly amounts ample enough to feed a family of twelve.

And once in a while he would feel himself so full of steam he'd try to hug or dance with my mother. But she always pushed him away.

Within that perpetual bustling about our house, I never saw my parents embrace or hold hands.

⁂

I almost forgot. I used to get sick. I used to have to stay home and not go to school because I was sick. I had asthma. I had bronchitis. I had fever. And my mother was a registered nurse.

When I got sick she would stay home with me. She did not disappear into her work at the hospital. She stayed home with me. She cut scraps of rough wool and, after rubbing my chest with Vicks VapoRub, she'd flatten that scratchy woolen square on top of me and button my pyjamas over that new insulating layer, and I felt absolutely peaceful.

My father barged in and out of the room, checking on my "progress" and asking about my temperature and insisting upon peeling an onion, cutting it in half, and jamming it into a jar of water from which the most obnoxious smell would soon begin to rise, and he'd be very pleased with himself, saying, "You can smell that? You must be getting better!"

I got to read all day long, propped up on pillows, and my mother would sponge bathe me and take my pulse, and sometimes I would finally be able to breathe deeply enough to doze off, and when I woke up sometimes I'd see my mother sitting near my bed, smiling at me.

⁂

I only used to get sick after we moved to Brooklyn.

⁂

Saturday morning was military and dense with arguments and contrary commotions and chaotic haste and fifty-seven plans and a hundred revisions and nevertheless the cleaning got done and a week's supply of food got bought and put away.

Then I'd hold my father's hand as we traveled all the way back into Manhattan, by trolley and subway, to the Museum of Natural History or the planetarium or the zoo or Rockefeller Center or Radio City Music Hall.

※ ※ ※

The first time my father took me to a symphony orchestra concert at Carnegie Hall, it was dark. I was so excited to be up and out of the house at night! I was stunned by so many grown-up people up and outside in the dark. I just couldn't get over it! Were they all going to the concert? What was about to happen?

And was that was that was that the moon?

Oh, I was so excited! What was going to happen?

My father kept saying, "You'll see! You'll see!"

And finally we got there and it was very very crowded and I was afraid I would lose my father but I didn't and we got to our seats and I couldn't see anything if I sat down so I stood up and then the concert started and I was looking at all these different men wearing black and white and playing different instruments together and I was about to explode with so many questions because I couldn't hear the music because the questions crashed around so loud inside my head but my father put his finger to his lips so I'd keep silent and after a while I crawled into his lap and fell asleep.

⁂

Sundays we rose even earlier than usual, consumed a quick breakfast, and walked the half mile to Brooklyn's St. Phillip's Episcopal Church. I loved this church. I thought it was the most beautiful, hallowed space. And beforehand my mother would spend extra time on her minimal ablutions and she'd fidget a hat onto her hair and, rather solemnly, we'd take to the streets, a familial but awkward-looking trio. I'd notice the agreeable smell of coffee and toast still clouding my mind, but I'd be clear about our destination. We'd find tons of other children and their parents when we got there, and everyone would be acting very friendly and very formal, and the vaulted interior of the church would let all of us feel little and close and glad of such deliberate company.

My father's Sunday preparations were quite a bit more complicated. He shaved himself with a straight razor, releasing a steel blade six inches long. But before anything else, he'd spend ten minutes sharpening that blade on a "razor strap" of broad leather hanging from a bathroom hook. And while he slapped the blade this way and that against the strap he'd be singing a calypso song, trying to scandalize my mother, who often pretended she could not hear him.

In fact, you could not help but hear my father.

And after the sharpening of the razor blade, he'd unearth his "finest English bristle" shaving brush and slurp it around in a small crockery bowl of shaving soap and create a creamy, almost bubbling lather, which he'd then lavish all over his cheeks and frequently all over mine.

Then there'd be complete silence. He was now actually shaving himself, and there would be no more songs and no more horsing around until he was done and that blade had been folded and sheathed safely out of sight.

At last he'd emerge from the bathroom, beaming, and ask me to examine his skin: Was it smooth? Was it soft? It was.

Well, then, would my mother care to give him a little kiss?

She would not.

"The Lord be with you."
"And with thy spirit."
"Let us pray."

Week after week I waited to hear those three lines, again and again. Who had composed such magic?

Before us stood the priest, his arms lifted up, his garments sanctified, silken, and regal, and below him we stood or kneeled as one body with one voice.

This unison amazed me. The oral structure of Episcopal litany calmed my heart and stirred my soul, and nobody had to try to teach me the meaning of that most mysterious Scripture:

> In the beginning was the Word
> and the Word was with God
> and the Word was God.

Did I not see and hear the truth of this assertion? Did I not long to live that truth with every fiber of my being? Did I not believe and desire and trust that truth, without understanding anything beyond the sound and the form and the consequences of that sound, that form?

It was so quiet!

There were no arguments, no cigars, no sarcasm, no jangling oddities or dangers.

I felt safe.

Everyone stayed on company behavior, or better than that.

And the stupendous height and depth of the church imparted a sense of infinite, imperturbable shelter.

Who would ever dare to desecrate the House of the Lord?

And, as my body was the temple
of God, who would dare to attack
or defile me?

"For He shall give his angels charge over you,
to keep you in all your ways."

And what about God's only "begotten" Son?

And what about the literal sip of literal sweet
red wine from the golden goblet
of Holy Communion?

"Yea, though I walk through the valley
of the shadow of death
I will fear no evil
for Thou art with me."

And what about God, who would "smite"
my enemies?

Who were my enemies?

⁂

I could never get enough of it: Church. I had mixed feelings about prayer, especially my mother's prayers, which were so specific and so apparently oblivious to whether anybody heard or "answered" them. But church was different. Church was undeniable. A good part of the time I was not sure what anybody was talking about, but no one seemed to care about that:

What mattered was the magical language and its repetition that left you feeling united and taken care of, and happy "in the Lord."

The entire congregation used the same words to invoke and preserve that magic, and so I learned those words: I savored and I repeated and I longed for and I thought about and I dreamed about:

> "The Lord be with you."
> "And with thy spirit."
> "Let us pray."

I imitated the monotone but rhythmical incantations of the priest. I memorized the patterns of his call and our response. I prided myself on being the first one down on her knees.

I was eager to prove my deference, my willing belief. It was stunning to consider that one word—for example, the very name Jesus—could make the mighty bow down and the crippled rise up and walk.

Just thinking about "Jesus," I grew dizzy. I felt intoxicated.

This was Sunday worship for the fellowship of Christ. None of that translated into anything I understood, except for the concept of worship, which seemed to be something contagious and exalted and extremely satisfying, even if specific to nothing known or visible. Worship felt to me like a relief from anything regular or ordinary. I suspected that was the point. I was wild about worship.

Best of all was the altar. Framed by stained-glass paintings, there it stood, shimmering and hushed, the gold cross hovering above a marble mantelpiece with elongated, lit candles held by gold candelabra surrounded by massive and fragrant floral displays.

Actually, if I'd had to name the four most mysterious and provocative ideas or facts I had run across by my sixth birthday, I'd have said *dinosaurs, Indians, diamonds,* and *God.*

But I only ran smack into God at church.

Suddenly the organ would vibrate its overpowering chords and triads into an irresistible summoning that meant we should stand up for the Processional.

And then, while everyone stood in the pews, singing—

In Christ there is no East or West

in Him no South or North
But one great fellowship of Love
Throughout the whole wide world.

there would begin the most familiar and reliable and fabulous parade from the back of the church to the front.

Wearing white gloves and a starched white cassock, first, would come the acolyte with a gold-chained chalice of incense that he swung from side to side to perfume and sanctify the air. And then would come the second acolyte, also white-gloved and cassocked, and he'd be marching forward, dead-step-military, holding aloft a gold cross about nine feet high.

Behind him came the priest, our Father Coleman, who in fact lived on our block and was the first Black man ever to sit on New York City's Board of Education.

He was a rather tall, very handsome, brown-skinned man who evidently chain-smoked cigarettes, and so he was forever coughing and spitting into the snowiest of white handkerchiefs. Behind Father Coleman came the choir in full-length blue robes and starched white collars, and behind them walked the all-important deacons of the church who always carried themselves like prissy funeral undertakers.

I liked the slender candles and the singing in unison and the pervasive incense, and although I had never seen a movie, I thought Father Coleman looked like a movie star.

⁂

When it was wintertime I got to use my Sunday velvet muff to keep my hands warm on the walk to and from St. Phillip's.

It was dark brown and stuffed in some absolutely soft and cuddly way, and I'd poke my hands inside my Sunday muff and never worry about a thing.

⁂

It's a summer morning. It's 10:30 A.M. With my coloring book and crayons, I'm bent over the kitchen table. And I'm sniffling from a cold.

On top of the radio on top of the roto-broiler on top of the utility cart, there are five enormous grapefruits. Over the radio, a white man winds up his lecture:

> "What can be done? What can you do? What can anybody do to stop the washing away of Vitamin C *even* as you drink citrus fruit juices to replenish your Vitamin C supply? *Is* there an answer? Can you come up with one?"

Here my father makes his surprise move. He bangs his fist on the cart. The grapefruits roll off every which way.

"Well?"

I lift my head to look at him. My crayon drops from my

fingers. I lower my hands toward the back of my chair so that I can push away from the table, fast.

And I make sure to answer him,

"Yes, Sir?"

"Yassuh! Eh! You don' hear the mon ask the question? Heh? Vitamin C, girl: Vitamin C! How you gwine keep it in the body?"

"I don't know, Daddy."

"Aghh! You don' even try. What you tink? You tink the mon's a fool! You tink the mon talk to hear himself talk! You tink you must be too smart to learn from the radio! Too smart to learn from an ignorant mon like me, you father! You one of these know-it-all wiseguys, heh? You know even an old mon like me must be making himself learn? Even when the white, the young boss him get on the elevator—you tink I closing my ears? You tink they say anyt'ing an' I don' make myself listen what it is?"

"No, Sir."

"Speak up, Mon! You hear me talkin' to you, don't you?"

"Yes, Sir."

"'Yassuh, yassuh': That all you know how to say to me! You tink this is the Army? If this was the Army, believe me, girl, you won't be sit there holding a crayon! Let me see what you got there!"

He jerks the coloring book away from me:

"Hmmph. Roy Rogers. On horseback. Now, that's good: How the West Was Won; you ever tink to yourself How Did the United States of America Get So Big? Boy, it's a vast one, you know!

"That was the frontier! It took strong men, men of faith! Men of courage. To go out there—*into the unknown*—an' fight everything—the climate, the wolves, the Indians—everything! An' fight *to win* a victory! A place to live! A place to be a mon."

I should agree or cheer for "The Frontier," but I don't know how.

"Look at the damn garbage of Brooklyn. They tink because this is a Negro neighborhood, they tink we like garbage, they tink we love garbage, they tink we need the garbage so we can feel at home!"

He smashes the garbage can cover down on its contents:

"I gwine call them up Monday an' give them something to hear! Where is your mother?"

I shrug my shoulders.

He rushes at me. He yanks me up from my seat. He shakes me:

"Where is your mother gone?"

"I don't know, Daddy."

"That's better. I ain' raise no hellion around here. There don' be no disrespect while I am head of this house! I have enough of that foolishness up on the job! The white boys them in a suit and tie an' calling me—old enough to be the father—calling me 'sonny,' calling me what they damn please: Hmmph!"

I reach for a Kleenex.

"Ahh. You got asthma. You got runny nose. You growing up soft, girl. I gwine send you away. Maybe to New Jersey. And make you healthy yourself: Let you breathing clean air, clean air. Harden you up!"

He grins at me:

"I gwine buy you some Vitamin C *tablets*: Put *hair* on you chest!"

He puts a hand on my arm:

"Listen to me, girl. Mon to mon: You see? You have to be tink to you'self about *everting*. You can' go through life like a nincompoop. You have to use you coconut!"

He thumps my forehead. I think this is a good sign:

"Daddy, can I please go out?"

"Yes, you *can*. But no: You *may* not go! You remember what I tell you about *can* an' *may* do? Hmmph. The Brooklyn street is not going anywhere.

"Do you believe that? Do you believe that even if you don' go to the street before *tomorrow night* it will still be there, waiting. For what? Waiting to suck you down, girl. Heh? You *may* go out this afternoon. But now I wan' that you go upstairs an' wrestle wit them books!"

"But I finished the reading, Sir."

"What! You finish the whole of *The Merchant of Venice* by Mr. William Shakespeare?"

"Yes, Sir."

"An' did you make sense of it, mon?"

"No, Sir."

"Aha! Then you read it again an' you read it again until you thought through what it mean! An' what about the poem?"

"I couldn't finish all of it."

"Let me hear what you did get to!"

"'If you can keep your head while all about are losing theirs— If you can dream—and not make dreams your master—'"

I lose track of the lines.

"That can' be right! G'wan with yourself: Upstairs an' study it! G'wan!"

I try to get out of there.

"'Tention!"

I freeze.

"Head up! Shoulders back! Stomach in! And don' be shuffling, girl. You ain gwine be no run of the mill *Negro* sneaking around. You gwine be a fine mon you must be walk like a mon. I want that you stand tall an' *stride* ahead! Strut your stuff, girl! G'wan! G'wan!"

"Daddy? Around here, nobody walks like this!"

"An' so?"

"The other kids—it'll look funny. I only see white people walk this way!"

"That should tell you someting! If the white people do it, you better to study yourself how it goes! G'wan! G'wan! Wait!"

I halt. My father executes a caricature bebop step around me:

"You like to see the old man cripple himself up like this? Looking *sharp,* heh?"

He makes me laugh.

"What you suppose you do now? A chimpanzee? Why you gwine cover up you mouth? When a *mon* laugh him throw him head *back* an' laughing out *loud*!"

Suddenly my father shouts:

"Tink fast!"

He fakes a punch at me. I am cowering, but he feints a left jab or two. I make a mistake: I look away. Then my father fakes a knockout punch to my face. He catches his fist half an inch away from my forehead. I'm looking up at him now, for sure.

He laughs:

"Don't I tol' you you don' never take you eye off the enemy eye? Never! Hmmph! You see now, heh?"

He smiles at me:
"G'wan now; *upstairs*!"

❖ ❖ ❖

Daddy at the stove or sink. Large
knife nearby or artfully
suspended by his clean hand handsome
even in its menace
slamming the silverware drawer
open and shut/the spoons
suddenly loud as the yelling
at my mother.
No (she would say) no
Granville no
about: would he
be late/had she
hidden away the Chinese laundry shirts
again/did she think
it right that he (a man in his own house)
should serve himself a cup of tea a plate
of food/perhaps she thought that he
should cook the cabbage and the pot roast
for himself
as well?

It sure did seem she wanted him to lose
his job because she could not find
the keys
he could not find
and no (she would attempt to disagree)
no Granville no
but was he
trying to destroy her with his mouth?
"My mouth?!" my daddy hunkered down
incredulous and burly now
with anger, "What you mean, 'My Mouth'?! You, woman!
Who
you talk to in that way?
I am master of this castle!" Here
he'd gesture with a kitchen fork
around the sagging clutter
laugh and choke the rage tears
watering his eyes: "You no to speak to me
like that: You hear?
You damn Black woman!"
And my mother
backing up or hunching smaller
than frail bones should easily allow
began to munch on saltine

crackers
let the flat crumbs scatter on her full lips
and the oilcloth
on the table.
"You answer me!" he'd scream, at last:
"I speak to you. You answer me!"
And she might struggle then
to swallow
or to mumble finally out loud:
"And who are you supposed to be? The Queen
of England? Or the King?"
And he
berserk with fury lifted
chair or frying pan
and I'd attack
in her defense: "No
Daddy! No!" rushing for his knees
and begging, "Please
don't, Daddy, please!"
He'd come down hard: My head
break into daylight pain
or rip me spinning crookedly across the floor.
I'd match him fast
for madness
lineage in wild display

age six
my pigtails long enough to hang me
from the ceiling.
I would race about for weaponry
another chair a knife
a flowered glass
the radio.
"You stop it, Daddy! Stop it!":
brandishing my arsenal
my mother
silently
beside the point.
He'd seize me or he'd duck the glass.
"You devil child!
You damn Black devil child!"
"And what are you supposed to be?"
my mother might inquire
from the doorway:
"White? Are you supposed to be a white man
Granville?"
"Not white, but right!" And I would have to bite
and kick
or race away
sometimes out of the house and racing
still for blocks

my daddy chasing
after me.

❖ ❖ ❖

Daddy at the table reading
all about the Fiji Islanders or childhood
in Brazil
his favorite National Geographic research
into life beyond our
neighborhood
my mother looking into
the refrigerator.
"Momma!" I cried, after staring at the front page
photo of the Daily News.
"What's this a picture of?"
It was Black and White,
But nothing else. No people
and no houses anywhere. My mother
came and took a look over my shoulder.
"It's about the Jews," she said.
"The Jews?"
"It's not! It's more about those Nazis!" Daddy
interjected.
"No, Granville, no!
It's about the Jews. In the war going on,"

my mother amplified, "the German soldiers
take away the Jewish families and they make
them march through snow until they die!"
"What kind of an ignorant
woman are you?" Daddy shouted out, "It's
not the snow. It's Nazi camps: The concentration
camps!"
"The camps?" I asked them, eagerly: "The Nazis?"
I was quite confused, "But in this picture,
Daddy, I can't see nobody."
"Anybody," he corrected me: "You can' see
anybody!" "Yes, but what," I persevered, "what is
this a picture of?"
"That's the trail of blood left by the Jewish girls
and women out on the snow because the Germans
make them march so long."
"Does the snow make feet bleed, Momma?
Where does the bleeding come from?"
My mother told me I should put away
the papers and not continue to upset myself
about these things I could not understand
and I remember
wondering if my family was a war
going on

and if
there would soon be blood
someplace in the house
and where
the blood of my family would come from.

part three

DEEP SEA FISHING AND THE BEACH

I think we got closer to the ocean when we left Harlem.

My father began to acquire a variety of fishing rods and lures and hooks and lines, and he kept what he called a tackle box, on a shelf I could just about reach, in the shed between the kitchen and our backyard.

I liked looking at the lures: Glinting silver, iridescent feathers, and a hollow, bobbing sphere, half white, half red.

It was fun to imagine fish interested by something unfamiliar and shiny. Or not interested.

It made them seem more like elusive household pets and less like creatures you should kill and eat.

My mother began promoting a trip to the beach.

She said it would make for a good family outing. We would leave the house behind us. We would get some sun. I might learn how to swim. And she'd cook.

But it had to be summertime before we could go. Otherwise, she said, we would not enjoy ourselves.

I wanted to know if the water was nearby.

Both my parents told me it was "not too far away."

I couldn't really picture it.

* * *

In my favorite book, *If I Were Going,* there was a chapter, "It Happened in Brittany," which described the fishing adventures of Yvon, a boy about my age.

He'd sneaked himself onto a fishing boat that belonged to a man named Pierre. They'd caught an amazing amount of sardines, but then the wind had died down and so the boat had stalled way out at sea.

That was a lot of upset, because Yvon's mother had no idea that her son had boarded a ship and sailed away, hoping to find sardines.

She didn't know where he was.

Time passed. Then the wind picked up, the sails got full of air, and the fishing boat headed homeward, loaded with the great big catch of squiggling fish.

Yvon's mother was so excited that she stumbled as she ran to the end of the dock. But soon she could see little Yvon standing next to the mast. So she stopped worrying about him.

And she was so happy. And everybody else was so happy about the sardines.

Yvon didn't have to explain everything.

So one thing I learned was about the wind. You needed it not to die down.

But it was unpredictable.

In another book, Donald Duck was Huey, Louie, and Dewey's uncle, and he wanted to take them to the beach. But mostly the story centered on a wooden picnic basket that held a certain number of bologna sandwiches with lettuce leaves sticking out, and Huey, Louie, and Dewey did not want to share the sandwiches equally among themselves, and Uncle Donald became quite exasperated, and I could never remember what finally happened. And there was not a happy ending, as best I could recall.

⁂ ⁂ ⁂

I must have been six when my first fishing adventure began to seem unavoidable.

My father cajoled me into trying out different rods until he decided which was the right weight, flexibility, and length for me.

Then he sat me down and explained that we'd go deep-sea fishing in a few days.

The deep-sea part meant that I'd have to be very, very careful not to fall overboard. We'd be moving, then anchored, in water deeper under the surface than our house was high.

He waited, watching me for a reaction. But instead I asked for clarification:

"If I fall overboard then I'll probably drown?"

My father confirmed my fears.

So I asked him, "But what will I hold on to?"

My father said I could hold on to his leg or the outer railing of the boat's deck.

The trick was simply to hold on tight.

⁂

Because my father boasted that deep-sea fishing would help to "make a man" out of me, I was pretty sure my mother would not be coming along.

She'd stay behind, like Yvon's mother, and worry until we got back.

⁂

I felt considerable dread about this upcoming expedition.

My father had explained to me how early he'd have to wake me up: Two o'clock in the morning! It would be dark still, and extremely cold.

Because I knew my father would be the one rolling back those heavy mahogany doors that protected my narrow sleeping space, I felt that deep-sea fishing might begin with my father's fist smashing into the side of my head. So no matter how much I tried to calm myself with the thought that this particular impending wake-up might mean only that I needed to wake up, I hardly slept during the next two nights.

In case my father decided to attack, I didn't want to be sound asleep.

In the middle of the second night, I heard him coming up the stairs. I pulled the covers close and lay there, tense, with my eyelids jumpy but shut.

He rolled back the doors and the rumbling sound they made matched the trembling of my body.

He switched on the overhead light and, in a clearly jovial mood, boomed out loud that I should "Rise and shine!"

So I did.

As hastily as I could, I followed him downstairs and swallowed a sip of his sugary coffee, which he offered me, as an obvious treat, in a tablespoon.

I half expected that I'd have to consume a disgusting "hearty breakfast," as well. But to my surprise, my father said it would be best for me to travel on an empty stomach.

All over the kitchen there were sacks of things and the tackle box and three fishing rods and a thermos bottle and my lunch pail.

I was to carry my lunch pail and my fishing rod. He'd manage the rest by himself.

My mother appeared, looking quite sleepy and not inclined to enter into any conversation with my father.

She dressed me in multiple layers of clothing, and then my father, oblivious, changed what I was wearing to suit his own ideas and at the last minute fitted one of his baseball caps over my hair and the tips of my ears.

I couldn't see very well, but he said that was just fine.

My mother asked him to reconsider and let me stay at home.

My father put down whatever he'd been lifting and stared at her.

Then he picked everything up, showed me how to reorganize my lunch pail and my fishing rod so they wouldn't encumber me, and told my mother that what she could do was open the gate for us and then lock it after we'd gone.

By now it must have been almost 3 A.M., and we were hurrying to see the sun rise over the ocean.

So we hurried down the block in silence.

And we waited for the bus. And then my father decided we'd walk along, rather than freeze up standing still. So we walked along until we saw the headlights of a bus approaching us. And my father ran ahead, and I ran after him, to board the bus at the next corner.

Then we got off and walked to the Long Island Rail Road station and waited for a train. Then we boarded that train and then we started to travel really fast.

And I didn't feel tired at all.

The train kept speeding away from Brooklyn and streets and houses and darkness.

Outside the windows, the glimmering of a soft, sweet, golden light began to alter everything.

And when we got off, I couldn't see anything specific or recognizable.

But my father held my hand and ordered me to run some more, and so I ran with him, and then he said we'd just make it.

And we made it.

We boarded a fishing boat entirely full of men.

And the engine shook below the deck and the shallow waves rocked the boat side to side and my father seemed ecstatic when he found a spot for us at the outer railing and set up our gear.

The boat began to slide away from its moorings and I could smell gasoline and pipe tobacco and things the men were drinking out of bottles and pocket flasks and my father was just grinning as he put his arm around my shoulder and told me to breathe in and breathe out.

Repeatedly he exclaimed, "This is the life!" and "You to hold on to me now!"

And when the sun finished rising into the sky, it was the God's truth that the world had changed and everywhere around us had become the deep blue sea.

* * *

Preparations for a day at the beach began seventy-two hours earlier. My mother turned and turned around the kitchen. There would be layer cake and cupcakes and maybe apple pie, plus a gallon of lemonade and a couple of quarts of grape juice, just in case.

Then there were the many things she'd ask me to "test" as she proceeded with her circular preparations: Was there enough pepper in the potato salad? Enough salt? And I must not let her forget to pack plenty of plums and grapes and peaches!

And, not to neglect our protein requirements, I could even listen to the sizzling grease into which my mother dropped one piece of heavily floured chicken after another, and then another, until an irresistible mound of fried chicken teetered at the edge of the stove, which on a back burner hard-boiled two dozen eggs that, later on, my mother would "devil" with hot sauce and relish and minced onions and much mayonnaise.

While my mother worked until beads of sweat stood on her upper lip and rolled down the sides of her cheeks, I'd be sitting at the kitchen table trying to memorize a Paul Laurence Dunbar stanza about dressing up for a party or a Shakespeare sonnet about some lady more lovely than a summer's day and wishing we had an electric fan.

We didn't have one.

On the worst hot nights, my mother might bathe me in almost-cold water and then sprinkle talcum powder on my neck and throat and then sit beside my bed, fanning me with a waxed-paper fan she must have stolen from our church because I only saw fans like that at St. Philips on Sundays.

And she'd say I was supposed to fall asleep while she was fanning me: That was the point.

But I wanted her to stay there beside my bed forever, and I'd do my best to not even get sleepy, and sometimes she'd laugh at our checkmate situation.

I'd do anything to see or hear my mother laugh.

Once she took me to the World's Fair, and I said, "Yes, thank you!" every single time she offered to buy me an additional sampling of all the world's food. I ate so much! My stomach was about to bust over the waistline of my shorts.

But I kept on eating and eating because she kept laughing, laughing, and laughing.

Mostly, she didn't.

But when she was getting things ready for our trip to the beach, now and then she'd sit down opposite me at the table and, smiling, she'd say: "We're going to the beach!"

And I'd be praying inside my head that it wouldn't rain, or something else bad, and ruin the day.

* * *

On the crowded deck of the fishing boat, there were no other children. The men certainly noticed me: "You brought along your little girl?" And my father answered them: "This is my right-hand man!"

So I knew I was supposed to make myself useful, but I didn't know how.

It seemed to take hours for us to get to wherever we were going, and I began to feel quite queasy, but my father urged me to just throw up, and if I didn't feel better, to stick my fingers down my throat and throw up again and again.

That would "purge" me. That would "cleanse" my "system."

He seemed really pleased at this purging prospect.

I was mortified.

And I threw up again and again, and my father pressed the palm of his hand against my forehead, I think to hold my brains in, and he encouraged me:

"That's it.

"That's good!

"That's good!"

I wanted to go home. My stomach and my throat and my head hurt, and so far I hadn't seen any kind of fish.

To distract me, my father demonstrated three or four switches on the fishing reels and explained the line motion each switch controlled.

Then suddenly the engine cut off. The boat began to heave up and down and up and down.

The captain announced that he'd sighted "a school" of

striped bass right under us. And just as suddenly, all the men, including my father, got serious and sober and busy.

Cans and jars of live worms and other live bait appeared and spilled onto the deck, which was now slippery for several utterly repulsive reasons.

My father insisted that I "master" the baiting of the hooks, and when I got a close look at them I thought they looked like small curved versions of Satan's pitchfork. They were horrible, deadly items, and I didn't want to think about what was going to happen.

Fishing was nothing but a big dirty trick!

You lured the fish with something pretty, and then teased them with something edible, and then they were hooked: Speared by these fiendish tiny wire contraptions that could slip into your flesh but would not slip out: They'd rip and tear your flesh apart, coming out.

They reminded me of something that made me cry. And I could see my father embarrassed by my tears. And so I tried to stop them.

* * *

I'm not sure how my father carried everything we needed, but he did.

Somehow he hauled along a beach umbrella, an umbrella stand, two blankets, a tablecloth, the food and the juice, money for the bus, and maybe money for popsicles and a box of Cracker Jack.

My mother folded one arm around a bunch of rolled-up towels and staggered ahead with the gallon of lemonade dragging down her other arm and shoulder.

No one carried me.

That was okay because I was carrying my color-coordinated shovel and pail for the sand.

And if Carlyle was coming with us, we'd hold each other's hand so we wouldn't "get lost."

It was not clear to me what "getting lost" involved, but I supposed it might be similar to a lost wallet or lost keys, except that wallets and keys did not have feelings of any sort.

At any rate, Carlyle and I liked holding hands with each other.

It reminded me that, someday, we were going to get married.

And I liked that, as well.

But getting to the beach meant riding the bus all the way into a strange white neighborhood and then waiting on the sidewalk under the sun until it was your family's turn to board the bus that took you to Jacob Riis Park.

That's where we were going.

And, for the occasion, my mother wore a "Chinese coolie" straw hat that rose to a point above the middle of her head, and which tied under her chin.

She kept her hair in two braids, up under that hat, with large hairpins.

She professed to feel cool in her freshly washed and ironed sleeveless cotton housedress. And she idled comfortably inside old nurses' shoes with the wedge rubber soles worn off on the outside of the heel.

You could see her bare legs with blue and green veins swollen here and there. And her eyes looked a little bit goofy as she persistently smiled and implored us to be patient and reassured us that, quite soon, we'd be able to get on the bus.

As we stood on that white neighborhood sidewalk, we found ourselves surrounded by white people also waiting for the bus. Some of the white people seemed to me quite young, and so I wondered where their parents were.

My father was holding everything together.

My mother was smiling.

I was not lost.

⁂

The deck became chaotic. The men were shouting. The fish were biting.

My father set me up at the railing, and no sooner did my line dip into the water than the line twitched and jerked.

"It's a fish! You caught yourself a fish!"

My father talked me through the reeling in of my prize.

My fishing rod bent into a semicircle, and it was hard to hold on to it.

Something really heavy was really agitated at the end of my line.

I was supposed to reel it in slowly, or else risk letting it twitch itself away.

Reel it in a bit, then stop. Then reel it in. Then stop.

Other men gathered around me, giving advice:

"Nice and easy!"

"Both hands on the rod!"

I was terrified I'd mess up and let the rod jump out of my hands. It was so heavy!

Was it about to snap under that invisible, wild weight?

At one point, my father changed a switch on my reel and then the line slowed down and you could hear a click-click-click as the line, inch by inch, reeled in.

Then there it was! A whole fish!

I kept reeling in the line until the fish dangled above my head.

My father reached out and cut the line and grabbed the fish with one motion.

He threw it on the deck. And it flapped and flipped there, gasping for air.

The men laughed and told me,

"You did that just like a boy!"

Everybody seemed proud of me and pleased.

My father dropped his line into the water and ordered me to "stand by!"

⁂

Once we got to the beach, the sand burned our feet and I saw more people spread out, everywhere, than I'd ever seen.

My father made a great show of pitching the umbrella deep into the sand and laying down the blankets under that shade.

My mother unpacked our family feast.

My father stripped down to his swimming trunks.

My mother raised the hem of her dress to the level of her knees.

To me she looked like a pretty lady, smiling and plump.

My father hoisted me over his shoulders and pounded down toward the water.

I could hear my mother calling after us,

"Gran-ville?!"

My father continued pell-mell into the ocean, and when he had waded several feet into it, he suddenly chucked me into the water.

I came up coughing and sputtering and scared.

But he lectured me:

"Only one way to swim! T'row you in the water!"

And next he demonstrated how I should turn my back on the waves and let them try to knock me down.

But now my mother had reached the edge of the surf.

She stood there as the sand under her feet sucked itself away.

She was still wearing that conical straw hat tied under her chin.

But she was wading into the water with a purpose.

She was not going to let her baby girl drown.

Even if she had to get her legs and the hem of her hitched-up housedress wet, she would intervene to save me.

Laughing out loud, my father sent me, splashing and collapsing and splashing and completely off balance, back to my mother, who wrapped me around in a towel and struggled with the dripping, awkward load of my body, back to our spot on the sand.

Then I wanted nothing more than to repeat the drama of water rush and rescue.

To make me stay put, my mother bribed me with paper plates of sandy goodies and paper cups of grape juice.

Beyond where she could see, my father was swimming in the ocean by himself.

If Carlyle had come along, he'd be knock-kneed and teeth-chattering and blue-lips cold inside another towel.

We were having a very good time!

My mother sat under the umbrella, trying to create a sand-free space and serving up deviled eggs and cupcakes, not in any particular sequence.

I never saw her eat much.

But there were moments when I saw her forget about the sand and just sit still, with her thin legs stretched straight out in front of her and her arms crossed over her bosom, and I'd watch her, sitting still like that.

And then I'd turn away to fill up my pail with sand.

* * *

If I had never thought much about fish before, I would never forget them after this!

Hundreds and hundreds of slithering fish landed on deck.

Sometimes a baby shark hopped about, thumping this way and that, until somebody hit its head with a hammer.

And there also were small fish that puffed up their bellies, puff and puff, belatedly hoping to protect themselves.

But mostly there were look-alike gray and striped fish gasping, gasping, and then dead.

My father said I had caught twelve fish, on this, my first time out.

He alone had caught more fish than we could possibly bring back to Brooklyn.

And the engine started up. And the men pulled in their lines.

And the boat turned toward shore.

And now I rested on a high, oily coil of rope while my father untangled our fishing lines and cleaned the lures and tossed the finally useless worms over the railing.

I couldn't help but observe some of the other men hacking off the heads of the fish, slicing open their undersides, and snipping off their fins and tails.

This incessant dismemberment made me want to sink into the ocean and never come back up.

I kept myself quiet. I counted it a blessing that at least they didn't bleed.

Ahead of us, the sun had begun to slip down a slanted stretch of sky, and I noticed the churned foam of the boat's wake and, past that, the vast and very deep blue sea showing no trace of fish or fishermen.

Looking about, I saw the chipped red paint of our boat's exterior, but I could not find a mast to stand beside.

And I did not believe my mother would be waiting at the end of the dock to welcome back my father and me.

part four

BOYS AND CATS

From my sixth birthday forward, my father said I was boy-crazy.

He had in mind to beat that out of me.

For sure, he did his best.

But there were so many boys!

⁂

I watched them play.

I watched them shoot marbles.

I watched them argue.

I watched them fight.

I watched them build roller-skate scooters out of fruit crates and scrap wood.

And I imitated everything they did.

My scooter took forever to construct, down in the basement.

And when I finally brought it outside, the thing refused to go anywhere except in circles.

I was humiliated.

But the boys on my block tried to fix it.

They turned it upside down and pushed out the rubber cushions behind my roller-skate wheels.

They switched the wheels from front to back.

They changed the position of the crate.

Nothing worked.

And I'd spent days building it.

But none of the boys made me feel bad.

It was okay.

I was okay.

The scooter was crazy.

⁂

One afternoon I was skating down the street. It was spring. I was warm enough and having a good time.

But suddenly the fingers of my left hand twisted into excruciating pain.

Somebody on his bike had come too close, and my fingers had caught in the spokes of his bicycle wheel, which continued to turn.

I screamed before I could think about it. And my fingers were bloody and mangled and I couldn't help crying right in front of everybody.

But I didn't want to go inside, because I didn't know what would happen. Maybe my father would beat me on top of my hand getting messed up like that. So I sat on the brownstone steps of our house, and I sat there crying.

And a bunch of boys gathered around.

And nobody knew what to say.

But Vincent Howard and Mike Douglas were two of the boys standing near me.

And Vincent said, "If she was my girlfriend I'd be kissing her fingers."

And I was totally crushed out on Mike, who at that moment looked like he needed to throw up just from the sight of my mangled, bleeding hand.

But Mike said,

"You wanna go with me?"

And I was so excited because I'd been liking him for two weeks.

So I answered him, "Yes!"

And then Mike leaned over and kissed my fingers. And all the rest of the boys laughed and cheered and I was feeling pretty swell.

But hours later my cousin Valerie cornered me inside the house:

"What is the matter with you?!"

And I thought she meant my messed-up fingers, but she slapped my face and, very angrily, she told me:

"Don't you ever say yes to some boy when he asks you anything! You make a fool out of me in the whole neighborhood!"

So then I said, "But I like Mike Douglas!"

And she screamed back,

"I don't care what you do or you don't do! But you never say yes to some boy! You hear me?"

I heard her. And I didn't get it:

"What was I supposed to say?"

And Valerie schooled me.

She said, "You say, 'I have to think about it.'"

⁂

About never saying yes to a boy, my father agreed with Valerie, except that she was teaching me style while he was selling me on the virtues of scorn.

Repeatedly he insisted on the lesson of the Apple on the Tree.

You didn't ever want to become an apple on the ground. Apples just lying there would begin to rot. Or somebody would step on them, crushing their pulp.

But if you hung there up on that tree—then! Then "the young man him must reach up high," and aspire to your elevated, inaccessible position. "Him must prize and pine for you."

This would mean striving, and therefore respect.

⁂

I did like boys.

In the first place, they liked me. They protected me. They never asked me to prove anything.

They never hurt me. They talked to me real nice. They never scared me, either.

Except for Oliver, who anyway was ugly, with bug-out eyes.

Nobody liked Oliver. He was just wrong.

He didn't even know how to be a boy.

For instance, he started a fight with me.

And that was ridiculous.

I was a girl. But here he was, waylaying me after school, punching at my head and punching my arms.

So I ran. But Oliver chased me.

And I ducked inside somebody's hallway.

But he caught me there.

And we fought.

I threw down my books.

And we fought hard.

He banged my head against the mailboxes until, just like in the comic books, I saw stars.

And then I got really mad.

I went for him.

I banged his head against the mailboxes.

I punched him where I thought his heart must be.

I punched him with a left and a right.

I banged his head against the mailboxes.

I wanted to kill him.

I could taste blood inside my mouth.

It was him or me.

And he was a boy.

And I was a girl.

And I left him there on the floor of the hallway.

I picked up my books and I left him right there.

Out on the street I felt dizzy and it seemed like a long, long way ahead of me that I had to walk by myself to get home.

So I sat on the curb.

I spit blood into the gutter.

I thought I must be dying.

I hoped Oliver was dead.

He could never get to be anybody's boyfriend.

* * *

Billy Brodnax was different. He was a really good friend of mine. In fact, he was like my brother, except that we always liked each other and never argued about anything.

One day I went skipping up the block and I saw Billy was doing something in the front yard with a broom. His father, Mr. Brodnax, was teaching Billy how to sweep.

I already knew how. So I said, "Oh! It's easy! Let me show you!"

But Mr. Brodnax intervened, "No, I'm showing Billy how to use a broom."

So I withdrew. And that's how I got the impression that it was not all right for a boy to learn anything from a girl.

⁂

My mother brought me into her little room.

I thought we were going to pray about something.

But instead she opened this pamphlet entitled "Growing Up?" and made me kneel beside her.

She told me that every little girl starts to bleed sooner or later, and that was normal, nothing to worry about.

So I asked her why I'd bleed and where I'd bleed from.

But she told me I'd know "when the time comes."

And that when it came, what I should do is stay very calm and tell her,

"The time has come."

⁂

I knew my time would never come with Sonny Beecham. He was so handsome and so lean and so mean I would've thought he should be a movie star, except for the fact that I'd only seen two movies, *Bambi* and *Isle of the Dead.*

⁂

Quite frequently, Sonny would be scheduled to fight some other boy. And we'd all hear about it and we'd be racing everywhere trying to find Sonny to trail him to the fight site.

At last it would happen. And we'd form this raggedy circle

around Sonny and the other boy and we'd start pushing and yelling. And Sonny would move around, slow and cool and deadly.

And the buildup dialog would more or less sound like this:

Sonny: "You got something to say to me?"

Other Boy: "I got more than that!"

Sonny: "What you got? Show me what you got!"

Other Boy: "I got your mother!"

Then Sonny would hit the other boy some kinda way. And the other boy would punch back. And it'd be on.

And we'd be yelling and pushing.

And Sonny would take his own sweet time.

But then one of the traded blows would solidly land and they'd both become furious, kicking and punching and angling for a hammerlock grip around the other one's head or throat.

And finally the other boy would crash, squirming and screaming, to the concrete.

And Sonny would yell,

"Say you're sorry!

"Say it again!

"You sorry?"

And he'd be about to pound the other boy's nose into the pavement, but he'd pull back and stand over the boy's body and say just one word:

"Punk!"

And then he'd leave.

⁂

Sonny was one of the two boys I only dreamed about.

He was too old for me. He came and went within a stratosphere where girls who might interest him would wear powder blue heels, like Valerie. I accepted these facts.

But I dreamed about him noticing me somehow, and maybe bringing me a pink frosted cupcake for my birthday.

My other dream was Ronnie Gumbs, who lived just a few doors down the street from Carlyle.

Ronnie was the older brother of Donnie Gumbs, who was intermittently one of my boyfriends.

Ronnie always looked like he needed to kill somebody.

I never saw him smile or make small talk.

He acted like he probably detested girls and things like paper dolls.

Or games of any kind.

And when the weather warmed up, I'd see him sitting on the stoop outside his cold-water tenement flat, sometimes for more than an hour.

And I'd wonder what he was thinking about or remembering, and I could never even guess.

⁂

I wasn't wild about paper dolls, myself.

Invariably, I'd cut the sleeve or the attachment tags, badly, and whatever it was would be ruined. And I'd try again, slowly, slowly, and botch the job again.

So at the end of a rainy day, there'd be nothing but iddy-biddy useless scraps of paper.

Marbles were different.

I never understood how you were supposed to play with them, but I'd carry my marbles to the big tree in front of our house and I'd scrape shallow ravines into the dirt, and pretty soon a bunch of boys would hover close by and we'd take turns rolling marbles and talking up one kind as against another. And the talk got quite interesting now and then:

"That's a big blue but ain'
no way you can
see through that big blue"
or
"I seen a grassy green
like that
one time
but mine's got dots
inside"

or
"You better to hold on to that milky
way because
seems like you don' wanna
let it go
even for a roller."

And I suspected that we were all making up a way to play with marbles, and I loved that, and finally one of the boys might choose two or three favorites as a present for me. He'd just let me hold the new marbles and keep them as my own.

And it didn't matter that I never learned the rules.

* * *

In my elementary school, P.S.26, there was one white boy. Maybe he was not the only white boy on the premises, but he was definitely the one I noticed, and even observed as best I could, without being, I thought, obvious.

Tommy Green and I sat in the same regimented morning space, day after day. He had red hair, freckles, green eyes, and he smelled funny; not funny, *ha-ha,* or funny, *bad*. But unusual.

He smelled like my grandfather's Camel cigarettes. I wondered if he slept in a hayloft or on a straw mattress. Either of those would explain the outdoor, fresh presence he seemed to exude.

So I liked standing or sitting next to him. His scent reminded me of children's stories I'd raced through: All of the children white and blond and rosy-cheeked, and generally busy at farm commotions like checking a bird's nest for speckled eggs or tracking a turtle under the barn.

But Tommy Green and I never spoke to each other. The occasion never came up. And I never got to ask him about his after-school activities.

But a land turtle with a speckled brown and yellow shell took to turning up in our backyard every year. And without hesitation I named it Tommy.

* * *

One reason I didn't like girls too much was Valerie.

But now and then she'd make me a tuna fish sandwich with onions and a huge amount of mayonnaise and black pepper, and she'd use white bread (which my parents did not allow me to eat), and I'd think she was just the best cousin in the world.

Or she'd imitate my father or one of our uncles or aunts and put me in stitches.

But mostly I did not like her too much.

I did not appreciate having to say "thank you" for her hand-me-down jackets.

I did not like her infinite contempt and her infinite superiority based upon how old she was, which was, as far as I could tell, not something she had accomplished by herself.

I did not like listening to how much her feet hurt in her newest pair of powder blue heels, or whatever.

But I could get even with her.

After she took me to see *Isle of the Dead*, starring Boris Karloff, I could terrify Valerie by lunging into her path and pretending to be a killer walking corpse. Or I could get hold of a dead rat or a dead mouse, still in its trap, and drop that in front of her and she'd freak.

Or I could tell her I'd heard really weird noises upstairs and we'd better hide under the sink, and we'd hide under the sink for hours, even though she was four years older than I. And the entire time I'd be about to die laughing.

* * *

I used to laugh all the time. I used to laugh so much and so hard in church, in school, at the kitchen table, on the subway! I used to laugh so much my nose would run and my eyes would tear and I just couldn't stop.

One of my elementary-school teachers warned me that if I didn't stop laughing all the time I would literally die laughing.

And of course I thought that was one of the funniest ideas I'd ever heard, and I just laughed.

❖❖❖

For whatever reason, my father and I never had a man-to-man conversation about sex. Instead, he broached the subject by saying, in a dangerously sarcastic tone of voice, that by now (I was seven) I must have noticed that there were men and there were women, boys and also girls.

He wanted to know if I'd ever thought about why that might be.

I had not thought about it.

So he told me that it was something to do with sex. And sex made people crazy. Some people lived for it. Others were willing to die for it. "It" was sex.

And the thing about sex was that the more sex you had, the more sex you wanted to have:

"But hear me, now, huh?!" he exclaimed; "All cats are gray in the night! You understand me?! All cats are gray in the night!"

I was completely dumbfounded. But apparently that was the end of the conversation.

❖❖❖

Mostly his head looked like an egg. And it was overgrown!

I didn't think he liked much about me, either.

His name was Earl.

He was eleven.

I was nine.

He was tall, and not silly at all.

We differed a lot.

But his parents and my mother thought we might be a good idea.

My mother said he was "a very nice boy."

He was "going places."

I knew what that meant.

And so, rather than provoke a ruckus, I allowed myself to make-believe a vaguely formal relationship with Earl, who mostly made me think of nothing more than zombie land.

Certainly, I did not feel anything.

But I was pretty annoyed by the breakfast-table pressure and, since the annual Young People's Fellowship Celebration was coming up fast at the church, I wanted to invent and pursue something else that would be entirely my own idea.

I decided to surprise everybody. I devoted myself to that surprise.

I especially wanted to shock Valerie, who had been studying with Katherine Dunham, and who had been showing off her versions of African-Caribbean dance for quite a while all over the house.

So I stole one of Valerie's 78s that featured a lot of loud and relentless drumming that I imagined must be extremely African. And then I secretly borrowed from my mother two long, gauzy, sequined black scarves and her one and only—her favorite—rhinestone necklace.

And, listening to that music, I began to act out my fantasy of an authentic African dance by an authentic African princess.

Since Valerie's frequent remarks about my clumsiness were true, this project required much embarrassing hard work.

But at last I thought I'd figured out a sequence of moves that seemed continuous and dramatic, and I got happy and impatient about my big surprise!

Somber Earl came over to escort me to the church on the night of my performance.

I'd be one of perhaps fifteen other children reciting poems or singing hymns or presenting short skits on a Biblical theme.

And if anybody challenged me, I was prepared to say I was Pharaoh's daughter just about to discover Baby Moses.

Inside the St. Phillip's parish house, the space was packed with families filling up the folding chairs and spilling into the aisle with restless offspring.

After the official program, there would be a dancing party upstairs for the "young people" so inclined.

I was ready and proud and bursting with jittery nerves.

Moments before my turn on stage, I raced into the bathroom and completely undressed. Then I tied one of my mother's scarves across my chest and her other scarf around my hips, letting the leftover length of it dangle toward the ground like a glittering veil of sorts.

Then, standing on my bare feet, I peered into the mirror and settled my mother's necklace on top of my hair so that the pendant lay exactly in the middle of my forehead.

I thought I looked really regal, really African, and I ran back into the auditorium and eagerly nodded to Earl, who placed the record on the phonograph as we'd agreed and, turning the volume way up, dropped the needle on the groove.

I went wild. I was dancing in the jungle. I was dancing in the desert. I was practically naked. I was free. I was laughing and whirling about and never losing the beat.

And then somebody stopped the music. And I could feel something awful. It was horribly quiet.

But I was not finished! What about the ending, the fantastic flourish I'd planned? I felt cold. I could suddenly tell how small I was, standing there. And I shivered; *I'm gonna get a whipping for this!*

I froze.

But then I made myself walk away, walk out of that awesome pit of disapproval.

And in my head I heard whisperings: *How could she do that?! How could she do that in church?* And so on. And so forth.

Nobody clapped.

And I put away my mother's things and returned to my ordinary clothes and went upstairs looking for the party.

On my way, I saw Earl, who pretended not to see me, and I hated him. At last I felt something for him: I felt hatred. He was, without a doubt, a complete flop as a boyfriend, breaking basic rules about standing up and standing down for your girl.

And I kept going, and I found myself crowded around by older boys I mostly didn't know, and I thought, *well, at least somebody liked it!*

And I personally wanted to start up the party by turning off the lights.

And this very cute teenage gangster named Cookie asked me to dance, and then Cookie told me Earl "must be crazy!"

Cookie said, "If you was *my* girlfriend, I'd be kissing you right now!"

And so I adored Cookie. And Cookie walked me home. And, sure enough, later that night, I got a whipping almost sent me to the other side.

I did like boys.

For example, an earlier Earl, Earl Boulden, who sat several desks behind me in the third grade, made me dream about butterscotch candy.

I thought he was beautiful in a butterscotch way. Wearing

one plaid flannel shirt or another, he'd sit with his solid shoulders, cleft chin, and thick, kinky hair and never utter a single word, even when the teacher called on him.

And I didn't think he was mute, because there was a different, special class if you couldn't talk or hear anything or see.

But anyway, he was all the time silent.

And once or twice a month he'd pass me a note with drawings of stick figures I'm pretty sure he intended to be sexual. There'd be a balloon for a head and then two sticks for arms and one stick for the torso and two sticks for legs with a lopsided balloon floating between them.

He'd write "me" under that. And he'd write "you" under the other stick figure, which displayed a big scribble of hair on top of the balloon that, apparently, he felt just fine about as a rendering of my particular head and my particular face.

I thought Earl was fascinating and also weird because he kept sending me pictures of sticks.

But besides these occasional notes, I knew Earl really liked me because every time I dropped anything—my pencil case, my eraser, my handkerchief, my notebook, my mittens, my mitten clips—he'd be right there, picking it up and handing it back to me with his smiling large brown eyes.

Best of all was one winter day.

I was stuck inside the house and miserable behind the wrought-iron bars protecting our ground-floor windows. I kept pacing about in my pajamas, my stupid bathrobe, and my corny red slippers.

It was boring! It was so stuffy!

I raised one of the windows two inches above the ledge.

I wanted to breathe fresh air.

And then he appeared.

Earl materialized in the front yard.

I stopped breathing.

It was him. It was Earl, for sure.

Under his cap with earflaps down, and scrunched under a large wool scarf and stumbling in gigantic galoshes over his shoes, it was Earl.

He hurried to the window and, seeing one of them open, reached into his pocket, took out a small paper bag, and pushed it through that opening.

The paper bag landed on the floor.

Earl turned and ran away.

I could hardly believe what I'd seen.

I stepped closer to the little bag lying there on the floor of a room of my father's house.

Tentatively, I touched it with the toe of my slipper.

It moved.

It was real.

I bent to pick it up, and I now could see his handwriting, in pencil: "For you," it said.

And it said, "From me."

I closed the door to the room. I rushed to a corner.

Than I reached inside that small paper bag. Thin strips of red and yellow and pink and blue, brand-new ribbons for my hair, lay there in such a happy, rainbow array!

I lifted each ribbon separate from the rest and looked at its color and felt its soft, shiny surface. Again and again, I held each one of those new ribbons between my fingers and showed it to the light of that still-open window.

And I forgot about everything else.

My father had given me a kitten once, and I liked the kitten-cuddling part of the deal, and I liked calling her Allegra because I knew that meant *happy.*

She was quite pretty, with pastel salmon stripes and a smudged nose.

But she was hit by a car and she died and I never wanted anything more to do with cats after that.

And then I read Edgar Allan Poe's story "The Black Cat" and I decided cats were really scary creatures, as likely to attack your eyes as they might be to purr against your ankles.

But our block was full of cats, stray cats.

And when a female cat went into heat, a gang of male cats would surround her and an incredibly disturbing exchange of yowlings would create an intensifying uproar for hours and hours.

Sometimes nobody could sleep. And neighbors would frequently open and bang shut their windows, hoping to frighten the cats and force their relocation.

One night, the yowling and intermittent snarls of competitive cat conflict landed right in front of our house. Protected by the hedges, there seemed to be hundreds of cats in full, operatic drama. The endless diversity of their uninhibited interplay was shocking, in fact, and completely distracting.

My father signaled me that I should follow him. So I did.

We went to the kitchen, where he filled the largest pot with water and put it on the fire to boil.

All the while he kept whistling, and indicated that my job was to watch the water.

So I did.

At last all that water bubbled at boiling point.

Now my father carefully lifted that unbelievably heavy pot, and I followed him up the stairs and into the parlor.

He set the pot down on the rug and quietly opened one of the windows wide.

Then he braced himself, lifted the pot by its side handles, and silently approached the windowsill. After allowing a second's pause to steady his aim, my father thrust the boiling water down on the cats below.

A most horrible cacophony of screams exploded into the air.

I thought I would faint.

The screams continued for a few minutes, and then there was no more sound.

My father stood at the windowsill, listening.

At last he closed the window and turned to face me.

"That's what you must do about that!" he said.

And then he told me,

"Now you can go to sleep!"

He meant "Go to sleep now!"

And I did try.

part five

CHOOSING, AND BEING CHOSEN FIGHTING, AND FIGHTING BACK

The reason we went everywhere by bus was because we didn't own a car.

We never owned a car. My father looked at cars as nasty evidence of a man not willing to make proper sacrifices for his children.

He could not imagine having money enough for a house and a car. You had to choose between them.

So that was that about cars.

But not about beautiful things.

Once a month or so, my father would dress up "like a million dollars" and vanish into the city, where he'd spend the day at art auctions at the Parke-Bernet Galleries. He'd only return home after purchasing odd items such as an antique Chinese vase, a hand-carved coffee table, or a fully restored Victorian hard-back couch.

One unforgettable acquisition was a tall, round terra-cotta vessel, intricately carved and visibly fragile, which soon held sidewalk brooms and snow shovels stuck between the two outer doors of our house.

He'd drill me about these incongruous possessions: They were things of value "because you see them beautiful, don't you?!"

But more than anything my father might say, I learned about beautiful things from what he did.

Night after night he studied seed catalogs. He compared

and calculated dimensions of dahlias and tulips and pear trees. And he planted and raised these flowers and these fruits with incredible focus and eventual success.

Our yard became an unmistakable locus for all of his yearnings.

Our garden, a surprising earthen horseshoe full of color and fragrance, curved around a concrete area he transformed by mixing regular cement with a dusky pink element that, in turn, diffused the meaning of "concrete."

He lectured me about "quality": Shoes, the fabric of his overcoat or suits—all were to be chosen for their value as beautiful things that would last.

And the first time I went to the Brooklyn Botanic Garden, he made me memorize the sign that read:

> Let it not be said:
> All was beauty
> until you passed by.

You needed to share and preserve beautiful things.

And my father's fastidious commitment to photography was his way of doing that.

He juggled a Rolleicord camera and a Rolleiflex, plus a modest caboodle of lights, light meter, tripod, and cables; these belongings gave him tremendous pleasure and grief.

And because he'd taught himself how to read, my father assumed you could master anything by "reading up" on the subject.

Nobody ever told him that learning, for example, how to fly a plane or operate a camera, strictly by reading about it was probably a route to failure.

So he continued to "read up" on photography, and never quite got it; he never relaxed into the actual "capturing of the moment."

Instead, he would triple-check exposure, speed, and distance, but if the object of these attentions happened to be a live human being, all of that preliminary fuss still might miss a genuine smile.

Nevertheless, he never retreated from his hopes of becoming "a natural."

And meanwhile, as a matter of fact, I accepted that anything beautiful required a good bit of work.

I grew used to watching my father interrelate a banana, an avocado, and the precious Chinese vase on a marble-topped small table that he must have bought precisely for these still-life compositions.

He'd place that table near a dining room window.

He'd adjust and readjust the Venetian blinds so that the incoming light shuttered the table's surface this way and not that.

Then he'd carefully poke at the Chinese vase until it stood where he thought it looked best.

Then he'd fool with the banana or the avocado or whatever else at the base of the vase.

Then, quite frequently, he'd travel all the way to a white neighborhood's supermarket in order to buy a truly beautiful banana, a truly beautiful apple, or nectarines.

Then he'd experiment with the height, the filters, and the angle of his camera lens.

And then he'd take his picture.

And I'd be standing by, riveted by the process of choice and consequence.

I'd never get bored.

And it did seem to me that just being chosen made you beautiful.

Apart from avocados, I'd become interested early on in being chosen, because of the Bible.

The Lord was always choosing people or choosing sides or choosing one person, a Hebrew prophet, as his spokesman.

If you got chosen as a people or a side, you'd win the battle or the mountain.

If you got chosen as a spokesman, things could get pretty frightening, in fact, before it turned out that you would prevail.

But in every case, it was the Word of the Lord that mattered.

He'd speak, and either you'd obey or you'd find yourself in fantastic, often fatal, difficulty.

The Word would "come down" from "on high."

Or there'd be thunder or a burning bush, and that would translate into more of the Lord's orders for the day.

And if you heard the thunder, then you had been chosen to lead inside a life-or-death context.

God's Word was nothing to ignore.

So I stayed interested in the stories about the prophets.

I wanted to be one.

But I never really thought that could happen.

I wouldn't be chosen.

I wasn't big enough.

Size was a sore point for me.

I was always so small that my schoolmates called me Shorty. And because I kept getting skipped out of one grade and into another, I'd always be the youngest one as well.

That's why I particularly loved Samuel.

He was just a little boy when God spoke to him, and Samuel thought somebody else was calling.

And that happened two times.

And then this older guy told Samuel to say, "Speak, Lord, for I am listening," and Samuel said that the third time, and then the Lord chose Samuel as his spokesman.

And because he was chosen, Samuel became really powerful.

And he was chosen because he heard the Word of the Lord.

And also there was Elijah. No one would give him the time of day. People made fun of him or forgot about him completely.

So Elijah was about ready to give up.

He needed the Word of the Lord to tell him what to do and to prove to folks that he'd been chosen.

So he ran away from everybody and tried to find a special place where the Lord could burn up a bush or whatever seemed necessary.

And there was a fire, but nothing happened
after that.

And there was an earthquake, but nothing
happened after that.

And then! Then God spoke to Elijah
"in a still, small voice"
and Elijah was really listening. And he
heard the Word of the Lord.
He'd been chosen.

And after that a lot happened, but it was all
okay for Elijah.

This way and that, I kept studying the Bible.
And I never got bored.
But school draws a blank.
I don't remember the names of any of my teachers.
I don't remember reading anything.
I do remember penmanship exercises, a map of
the world in Army camouflage colors, and
multiplication tables on the blackboard.
I do remember victory stamps "for the War."
I don't remember how we got the stamps
or what you were supposed to do,
besides paste them into a pocket-size
stamp pamphlet the teacher collected.
I hated school.

It always began with "a good breakfast" that, as my father became more and more "health-conscious," looked and tasted worse and worse: Runny soft-boiled egg on whole-wheat toast, wheat-germ flakes on top of that, and a glass of milk with Ovaltine stirred into it.

But there were compensations:

Liquid brown shoe polish I daubed all over my Buster Brown high-top lace-up school shoes: They'd glisten almost pink immediately, and that let me imagine myself about to wander into a magical mistake: A forest/a farm/a mountain trail.

And then there was my pencil box, which at the start of every semester I got to choose brand-new. It was often decorated with Mickey Mouse, and it was entirely mine.

Inside I'd find a serious-business pencil sharpener and long red or blue pencils, which I wanted both to use and to save. And I'd also find a boring, boring ruler. And I'd also always find a compass, which I enjoyed playing with, mainly because the teacher seemed unaware of its existence, let alone its homework potential.

School invariably ended with one big fight or a bunch of them.

As the minute hand of the classroom clock bumped closer and closer to three, my stomach would grumble and tighten up.

At the edge of our seats, hands folded on our desks, we waited for the words "Class dismissed!"

I'd stare past the teacher's head, trying to shrink my confusion about what would happen next:

Who was going to get beat up?

Was it going to be me?

I never asked, "Why is so-and-so going to get beat up?!"

I don't believe anybody ever asked.

And it never occurred to me that getting beat up meant anything passive about anything: It meant you just had to fight.

When school let out, it was that time.

And so nobody rushed into the street. In fact, we'd all exit as slowly as we could, pretending there was no hurry and no worry.

But just past the hurricane-fence boundaries to the schoolyard, somebody would jump in somebody's face or knock somebody's books to the ground or yank your head back hard, grabbing at your braids, and then it was on:

The pushing and taunting and, finally, the crunch of the punch to your nose, or the slap that made your head blink with blood.

In general, only the boys did the fighting, and that was fine because (everybody said) girls would scratch up your face and scratch out your eyes; Girls fought "dirty" because they didn't know how to fight. So, if possible, it was better not to fight with them.

And because our code of honor did not allow the boys to fight with the girls anyway, I personally had no choice about it: In general, if I was going to get beat up, that would mean I was going to fight some girl.

I'd just have to watch out for her fingernails.

* * *

In a way, fighting was a huge relief. So I didn't mind it too much.

Way more than maybe getting beat up, I hated being afraid of anything.

That was creepy in the extreme: Walking around scared.

And I felt that a lot,

because I never knew when my mother or

my father was going to hit me, or why.

I suppose I came home from school at very different times after three.

It depended on what kind of a fight lasted how long.

Even if you were not the one targeted for the main fight that day, you couldn't just sidestep the big action of your peers.

You were supposed to stay there, shoving and yelling, and also improving your own fighter abilities by observation. Plus, every single fight changed somebody's status.

And you had to catch that news as it went down.

Your own reputation would suffer or plummet if you didn't know, day by day, the winners.

But besides all this, I got into fights at school about once a week at least. And whenever I went outside the house to play for an allotted hour, or an hour and a half, that meant I'd be fighting:

Another little girl, or a group of other little girls, would insult or jump me, and pretty quick I'd be banging away with my fists and keeping my chin tucked down. If and when I actually got hurt, I'd suddenly go ballistic. Around where I lived, people said I had "a terrible temper" and that I was "crazy" if you got me mad.

At any rate, I seldom came home from school right away.

Maybe that's why they beat me.

I never had a wristwatch, so I seldom came home exactly after an allotted hour or an hour and a half.

Maybe that's why they beat me.

I don't know.

But I'd ring the bell sticking out of the brownstone beside the iron gate door to our house.

And I'd wait.

Then my mother would shuffle toward
the gate and click it open.
I'd step down to enter the house.
And sometimes, just as I'd be
coming in right past my mother, she'd
just knock me down. And I'd
cringe there on the concrete, waiting for the next blow.
But with my mother, there was never
a second or third attack.
I was down.
It was over.
And I never knew why about the whole thing.
I never hit her back. She was my mother.

And she was like a girl.

But with my father, the beating turned into a fight between us.

He'd start with a series of fake questions, and what I'd understand, basically, was that there was nothing I could say to derail his furious sarcasm and his gathering rage.

It seemed he needed to frighten me first with his words and his voice.

Then he'd rush at me, either by himself or with something he'd pick up as he lunged.

And he'd tell me I was being disrespectful if I didn't just sit or stand in place and make myself take it "like a man."

I was consistently disrespectful.

I ran. I ducked. I threw things back. I tried to escape.

Once I ran out of the house for several blocks in my pyjamas. And he chased after me and, at last, caught me and beat me—in public.

And he said now I should be ashamed.

But I thought he should be ashamed.

That was my opinion.

I did not like being picked on or

beat up.

I did not like things happening

to me out of the blue.

⁂ ⁂ ⁂

Toward the end of my seventh year, I took to sleeping with a knife under my pillow. So when my father rumbled those mahogany doors open and started to beat me in the middle of the night, I pulled out my knife and I asked him,

"What do you want?"

And I meant, "I'll kill you!"

And soon after that my father stopped

waking me up.

⁂ ⁂ ⁂

Actually, besides the Bible, I don't remember what I was reading, in general.

It must have been a huge pile of something because my mother said we'd used up our neighborhood library and so we shifted to a time-consuming weekly trek to the white neighborhood's library on Eastern Parkway.

My mother carried the books and I stared at the white people who smiled a lot at my mother and me.

She never took anything out for herself, or for my father, to read.

But in the front parlor of our house, there was an encyclopedia set of books and another set of stories with elephants and tigers and Sambo turning into butter, and since I often browsed among the gold-edged pages of these leather-bound volumes, I supposed that my parents did, too.

I knew that my father read voraciously. I saw him. I even saw him fall asleep with his finger still pointing to a word in a newspaper article or a magazine.

But he never neglected what he regarded as his prerogative and obligation: The training of my mind.

I do remember his reading assignments, because he'd test me every day.

Huckleberry Finn made no sense to me: Talk, talk, talk, and float down the river.

I disliked Tom Sawyer; I could see no excuse for a whole book about him.

Benjamin Franklin was a fat old man given to really peculiar activities.

And *Young Abraham Lincoln* left me cold. So what if they called him Honest Abe ?

And so what if he read his books by kerosene lantern or whatever?

I would, too, if I'd had a lantern like that, or "a roaring fire" to lie beside.

And as for his long walks to school? I noticed that he never got beat up: Never!

That left Rudyard Kipling and Shakespeare's plays and Shakespeare's sonnets and Paul Laurence Dunbar and Claude McKay and Edgar Allan Poe and Henry Wadsworth Longfellow and the Bible, supplemented by my mother's furtive teachings from *The Daily Word* and *The Book of Common Prayer*.

I liked classic comic books. I liked Robin Hood and Ivanhoe. I liked most of the moralistic illustrated tales for children that my mother kept for me near her costume jewelry, which I also liked to play with by myself.

Reading was okay. I was fast, so it didn't take forever. And it let me forget where I was and who I was and whether I was hungry or not.

Nobody bothered me when I was reading, except to make me eat or go to bed.

It was peaceful to read. And sometimes I could feel the words kissing my face; I would put my nose that close to the page. And because no one was watching me, sometimes I would just trip a word from the page to my eye to my ear to the page: THE. THE. THE. THE. THE.

So funny, I thought. Such a soft, funny thing showing up again and again! THE. THE. THE. THE.

I never understood the difference between "being angry" and "having a temper."

Apparently one of those was permissible and the other was not.

I had a temper. That was not good. But I had it nevertheless.

* * *

For "a poor man's vacation," my father packed me up, and he and I traveled out to the Shinnecock Indian Reservation.

I was pretty excited about the Indian part. And I pestered my father about what to expect.

Since we'd gone to the Museum of Natural History two million times, I was certain we'd stay in a teepee, and nobody would wear shoes or anything much besides feathers and beads.

And since we had always been West Indians, I wanted to know if they'd look like us, or what.

I was very glad I had very long hair that my mother had fixed into two very long braids for the occasion.

Perhaps I'd be given a beaded bracelet or a beaded ring!

For sure we would squat around a fire, listening to stories about bears and rain clouds and stars.

On the train, my father was not talkative. I wondered if he was getting mad or being angry or having a temper.

I thought I'd better keep my questions to myself.

But he lifted me to his lap and held me close. And he said that all that land you could look at from the train windows, all that land, all of it, belonged to Indians once upon a time.

But it didn't belong to Indians anymore. There had been a fight. The Indians had lost that fight.

They had lost all that land.

Now they lived on a beach on Long Island. That beach was reserved just for them. And it was fresh air and country, but it was just a beach.

That was all the Indians had left.

That's where we were going.

And there would be mosquitoes.

And there would be ants.

But there would be birds, too.

But not a lot of Indians.

⁂

I was so disappointed! When we arrived, an old pickup truck driven by an old man took us away from the train.

No ponies!

Nobody on horseback!

We bumped along a rocky, sandy road between extremely tall grass growing thick and wild, and ahead of us, through the fly-squashed, fly-stained windshield, you could see a clean blue sky.

My father tried to rally my spirits. He said we'd be able to play ball. There would be no traffic.

He said he'd be able to teach me to swim. There would be no waves.

He unwrapped a lollipop and gave it to me. I began to think vacation might be fun.

But when we reached the center of the reservation, I had to swallow hard.

No teepees!

I saw a handful of small ramshackle wooden houses with busted porch screens and broken steps.

I heard the buzzing of an ugly big fly.

Then some other people spoke to my father and me.

But they looked like folks on my block.

No different!

And because we were "guests," they said my father would have to stay in "The Men's House."

I would have to stay with some lady who tried to take my hand and tell me what to do.

But it was quiet.

Even when somebody said something,

it was quiet.

That was different.

But I cried when my father walked away from me "to put our things down," in "The Men's House."

I cried when that lady showed me the cot I was supposed to sleep on next to a gigantic bureau with a mirror that didn't work and no door to the room, just an opening in the wall where there should have been a door.

I just sat down and cried.

So the lady went and got my father. And he came and showed me around the reservation.

And I felt better.

And we found the "Ping-Pong Room," which was too small for the Ping-Pong table. It wasn't wide enough or high enough or long enough for real Ping-Pong. But it was a green table with a net and two paddles and a Ping-Pong ball.

So my father and I started to play.

We were having a very good time!

It was silly play because nothing fit right and I was still too short.

But then my father said we should switch sides.

And I was racing him to get to his
side of the table and a screw was sticking
out from the end of the net
and it caught my forearm
and ripped open the flesh to
the bone and I started to scream
and cry with shock and

pain and I punched and
I kicked the Ping-Pong table
and I tried to kill it. I
kept hitting it even with
my head hitting it and
hitting it because I
was hurt bad. I was
bleeding bad and
then
later when we got back
from the hospital
the men of the Shinnecock
Indian Reservation
held an "Elders' Council"
and they told my father that I
had "a really bad temper"
I needed to control or
I would get into big
trouble.
And the "Elders" told my father
to tell me
to stand in a corner
of the Ping-Pong Room
for half a day

until I got rid of my "temper."
So my father told me
to do that.
But I refused.

part six

MORE ABOUT MY FATHER AND MY MOTHER: FIGHTING

He lifts the machete.
WHACK!
He slices the grapefruit into two halves.
He's precise.
He washes the blade.
He dries it with the dish towel slung over his shoulder.
He puts the machete away.
He chooses another knife.
He uses that to free each section of the grapefruit.
He prods the seeds into the sink.
He gathers up the seeds and throws them into the garbage.
He runs water to clean the sink.
He devours each section, one by one.
He tilts his chin toward the ceiling.
He squeezes the grapefruit so the juice
streams into his eagerly open mouth.
My mother comes into the kitchen:
"Granville.
Why you can' sit down the table
and eat like a normal man?"

"Eh-eh? Mildred! You marry a backwoods barbarian an' now you want you have a gentlemon."

"Brooklyn is not a backwoods, Granville. All me want is. . . people to act. . . normal."

"But what you mean 'normal'? An I can' give a kiss to Mrs. Jordan? An I can' get a kiss from pret-ty Mrs. Jordan?"

My mother ignores his pursed lips and sits down:

"Oh, it is so hot an' humid! All me want is. . . to sit down an' let me stay put in one place! Too much commotion an' I can' concentrate!"

"But why you never have no get-up-an'-go. . . for you husband, heh?"

"Ah, Granville, believe me now: You gwine miss me if I get up one day an' I truly go away!"

"Hmmmph! What you talk about?"

My mother looks at him:

"But then again, maybe I don' really know about you! Maybe you don' need nuttin' at all besides you radio and you citrus fruit. . . . But where is June?"

"The girl gone upstairs to finish she reading."

"On a day like this?!"

"Have you never hear me say that Time Is Money? Boring you, eh? Why then do I have to repeat and repeat myself? You want that the child lay up around the house and then that get to be a regular routine: A training. What you training her for, Madam? What you tink she can do from the street, when the boy grown himself into a mon? Eh?"

"Ah, Granville! Don' bother me, mon, with s'more of your foolishness! I ain' talk now about no training for the girl. I mean to say the child is not a boy and the girl is still a child! And there *is* no school tomorrow and the sun is *out*: The other children them they already playing ball—"

"*That nigger riffraff*: What they do and what they don't do have nothing to do with my son, woman: *Nothing*! I'm not make all my sacrifice and save my pennies and spend me energies for the child to be like *what*—like me? The only ting I can do to get myself up in the world is to *what*?! Ride the elevator up and down the day long? You want him to come up like me? So he can marry *what*—some woman tink like you?! And live *where*—in a trashy neighborhood like this?!"

"I wouldn't talk that way if I were you."

"You are not me! See the color of my arm! You a *Black* womon: A monkey chaser down to you soul. I set you up here, something swell, in this house. Turn it over to you, and *what*? You wan' tie my hand. You wan' drag me down. You wan' throw that devil child to the street!

"Anyway: Him dark as you and coming up kinky-headed, too: Very well, let her go! Lock the door behind her!

"You damn Black womon: A mon home suppose to be a castle and see how me have to make me own something to eat!"

"But, Granville. . . . Don't I do everyting I can tink to

do. . . to have the child she growing on a straight and narrow path? Don't I do everything, Granville?

An' may God forgive me: But don't I even tell you. . . when you could *not* have otherwise no way to know. . . when it is that she may do something disobedient. . . . You wan' me to make some breakfast?"

"If it's not too much trouble, Mrs. Jordan! Ah, Mildred, you don' understand the world: You a womon. You a good womon. But you don't understand. I know what the child she have to face: She not gwine have you looking always after him. . . Millie.

"Do you realize the Rockefella children, from the moment they born, they belonging to the Rockefella family? You see? They don' have them no holiday from Rockefella life: They every day and night they learning: They learning to be Rockefella men: To be *leaders* of *men*: No holiday!"

"But, Granville. . .

"A Rockefeller boy *should* grow up to be a Rockefeller man! But we are *not* Rockefeller people. . . and June is not a Rockefeller boy! She have to become a Black woman!"

"Millie, never mind! Never mind about these tings! I don' know why you wan' talk to me about *people*: The child is *my* child, heh? I owe nothing to any man, Black or White, for the flesh of my flesh; I am *free* to do what I want."

"Granville. I met Mrs. Coleman at the greengrocer's this morning."

"Eh? And how is she husband? He gwine preach the sermon tomorrow? It *'tis* the *third* Sunday. . . "

"She tell me Father Coleman is feeling fine. She tell me you went over to the church. To talk with him. This week you did that."

"So. It's a free country, eh?"

"The child is just a baby, Granville! And she's an only one! Why must it be she have to be sent away!?"

"I know what I must do, Mildred: 'Tis the best boarding school in America! June she *will* rub elbows with the best: The sons of bankers! The sons of Captains of Industry!

"She will *learn* herself how to hold his own. She will come out the school a veritable prince. Among men!"

"But what do you mean: 'His own'? *Her own* is right here under your nose, mon! Under this very roof!

"How you can' see her own is *Black*, Granville, not white! The child is a *Black girl*, Granville; she can *not* change herself to white!"

"The child him my son! She have a name, *Jordan*. And him have another name, *June*! What you mean by *Black*? You want that she stay in the pits where they t'row us down here?!"

"Oh, Granville J.: Why you must love white people so?"

"Me! Love the white people?

"I love what the white people *have*! The house and the job and the garbage collection the good school and the policemon carrying the children them across the street!"

"Her own people, Granville, her own people!

"If we stick together. . . "

"Naw, Millie, it's a cage: A cage!"

"As a *group* we can make progress. . . "

"I don' wan' hear no more about it! *Progress!* You don' know, Mildred: You just don' see what you saying.

I am sick and tired to struggle like this.
Struggle is too slow!
Struggle is what they leave to the slaves!
I want the child walk and talking like a mon!

"I want her come to be a fighter and *win* sheself a life to be proud about. . . . Woman! I not gwine argue: My mind is made up! *This!* This place! This all of it! This! This is what she *have to* rise up above!"

"You gwine make her *afraid* to be sheself!
You gwine make her hate you, Granville. . .
if you don' kill her first
with you damn daydreams. . . "

He, my father, slaps my mother's face,
from one side to the other.
His hand stings.
He bellows loud bellowing loud
into that silence:
"You don' never belittle me, woman.
Or my love!"
I tumble down the stairs:
"Daddy! Daddy!"
"What you wan', boy?"
"Daddy. Would you like to hear my lines?"
"Okay, Little Girl. Ease you old mon's heart.
Give him a couple lines of poetry!"

"If you can talk with crowds and keep
your virtue,
Or walk with kings. . .
Or walk with kings. . .
nor lose the common touch,
If neither foes nor loving friends
can hurt you. . . .
nor loving friends . . .
Yours is the Earth and everything that's in it
And—which is more—
You'll be a Man, my son!"

"C'mere, you little monkey!

You listening to me?"

"Yes, Sir."

"What kind of ice cream is it that you think you deserve?"

"Chocolate, Daddy?"

"Okay! I gwine walk to the store now and buy some! You stay and help you mother what she need, eh?"

"Mommy, why! Mommy!"

"Never mind, now. Your father him have a lotta tings on him. . . . You listen what he say, you understand?"

"No, Mommy. Why?"

"'Why?' Because you do love your only father, hmmm?"

"*Yes*, Mommy, *no*!"

"You can' be holding hate for your father, June: In his heart of heart the sun rise and the sun set itself on you!"

"But between Daddy. . . and I feel. . . and I can't—Mommy, why? Mommy, *why*?"

"Shhh. It's all right. It'll be all right. . . ."

"What you lookin' at, eh?

Go an' make yourself useful!

Bring me the Bible!"

I go and I find the Bible.
I lay it across my mother's knees.
"Pull yourself up close, now.
This day: I wan' that you learn
something for me, June. And
for all time. . . .
You repeat it after me:
'Blessed are the poor in spirit.'"
"Blessed are the poor in spirit."
"'For theirs is the kingdom of heaven.'"
"For theirs is the kingdom of heaven."
"'Blessed are those who mourn.'"
"Blessed are those who mourn."
"'For they shall be comforted.'"
"For they shall be comforted."
"'Blessed are the meek.'"
"Blessed are the meek."
"'For they shall—'"
"Mommy, why? Mommy!"

part seven

MY GRANDMOTHER: HOORAY!

I called her Nanny.

She was my mother's mother. She was John Taylor's wife. She was the first lady of my life.

She'd always say, "Let the child be a child!" Or, "Leave the child alone!" Or, "But why you must fuss so!"

Rather than laughter, you'd hear her chuckling as she worked through a day, and you'd want to explore and expand the secret of that musical, happy sound.

My Nanny had the most enthralling thick lips that, just before the chuckle, stretched broad in a soft way I wanted to touch.

She never raised her voice.

She never wore anything besides immaculate church dresses and church dress-up shoes: Lace-ups with a one-and-a-half- to two-inch heel. For the outdoors, she completed her meticulous presentation with a Sunday handbag, and white cotton or black leather gloves, depending on the weather.

If the task of the moment meant baking or washing clothes, she'd simply add on an apron to protect her "good clothes."

And as far as I could tell, she didn't own any other kind.

I found her silver hair silky and thin, but early on I understood I should not "mess it up" by poking or pulling at it.

She wore rimless bifocal eyeglasses, and still she had trouble threading a needle. So I came in handy very often, as she was forever patching or darning or hemming or "stitching together" one thing or another.

The pinky finger of her left hand was permanently crippled up into a crooked position, and I thought that if I became a doctor when I grew up I would take care of that, I would remove that one imperfection.

Although: Without her glasses, my Nanny seemed to be practically blind; she'd bat her eyelids uselessly, and I'd notice a white ooze at the corners of her eyes, and I could never think what to do about any of that.

But she was never helpless.

Or bent.

Or stooped.

Sitting or standing, my Nanny's back held its proud, straight line.

And no one ever dented that conspicuous physical dignity, by word or deed.

No one.

She lived in an enormous four-story frame house in East Orange, New Jersey.

That house belonged to her because the white people she cleaned for gave her the money to buy it.

So she bought it.

And it was big.

And it was really far away from Brooklyn.

But we visited on holidays.

And I could never wait!

After too long we'd ring the bell and her husband, John, would trot down the stairs to let us in and, everlastingly, he'd be smiling and so tall and so slender and so handsome, in such a starched white shirt and such a pretty tie and dress-up trousers, and even as he hugged each one of us, he'd be calling up to his beloved wife: "Mah-ree! Mah-ree! But come! Look who is here!"

And Marie, my Nanny, would wait until we reached her at the top of the stairs, but behind her there would be a swirl, guaranteed, a feast of a lot of other relatives and neighbors, and a formally set dining room table complete with Irish linen tablecloth and sterling silver forks and knives and fourteen-carat-gold-rimmed Limoges place settings and candles and someone would be pedaling the player piano and somebody else would be handing around cigars to the men and John, or Tardy, as we children called him, would be pouring whiskey and chain-smoking Camel cigarettes and the visible excitement would be heightened by the most delicious smell of roast lamb or honeyed ham or roasted chicken and pies and cakes making their way to that ornate but impeccable dining table predetermined according to mysterious rules.

And what I noticed in the first minutes and then throughout those celebrations was how my grandmother, my Nanny, just about never let go of my hand, and nevertheless she stirred the gravy and teased my father about getting red-faced from one glass of sherry and told my mother to lie down and rest a bit and directed the placement of the forks and the platters and serving tureens of everything she had cooked herself, and finally, finally, took off her apron and, still holding me by my hand, brought everyone up short, to respectful attention, as some one of the men said grace, during which I would begin to giggle and to laugh, and I felt it didn't matter if I couldn't stop feeling so silly and tickled and full of so much giggling and laughter, and I was right.

It didn't matter.

She held on to me.

* * *

When I daydreamed about my Nanny, I saw sunlight on cornflakes and spoons, and I traced the repetitive squares of the oilcloth covering the breakfast table, and I wandered into the pantry and smelled cinnamon and curry and sneaked a slice of Wonder bread, or I sat in the parlor rocking chair, rocking with my head against a homemade snowflake doily, and I stared as John stood Sunday mornings in the middle of that exact room like a mannikin with his long arms extended while my Nanny adored him as she fastened his cuff links and pushed up the knot of his tie and brushed at the shirt seams covering his shoulders and he so comfortable and standing with a cigarette between his lips and no ash falling to the hand-waxed wooden floor.

When I stayed over by myself, my Nanny canned peaches from the gigantic backyard peach tree. Or rhubarb. Or she took down her rolling pin and flattened the dough for biscuits or she buttered my toast or brushed my teeth with a funny song to go along with the getting-me-ready routines to wake up or to sleep.

My grandparents never called each other anything but "Mah-ree" and "John."

They never said two words without saying "Mah-ree" or "John":

"You want me to give you coffee, John?"

"No, Mah-ree; no coffee."

I thought they pretty much liked everything about "Mah-ree" and "John."

They'd met on the job where John was the gardener for the same white people who employed my Nanny.

But I never saw him in a tee shirt or wearing a bandana like my father.

"John" and "Mah-ree" dressed alike: Seven days a week, ready for Christ Jesus Himself.

But my grandfather could fix anything. And nothing around my Nanny's house was broken.

One afternoon my parents came to take me back to Brooklyn. While they sat talking with Mah-ree and John, I went into the backyard and climbed the fence at the very back of the garden plot. Above the wooden boards, my grandfather had strung a couple of lines of barbed wire.

I reached for the lowest one and my footing slipped and suddenly I was hanging from the barbs of the wire: Knots of barbed wire pierced both of my wrists and I could not shake myself loose and the more I tried the deeper the barbed knots dug into my flesh and I screamed and screamed and a million minutes later my grandfather ran out and after assessing the situation he reached up and yanked my wrists free from the knotted barbs and I could not believe how much that hurt and I could not believe how much it kept hurting me and how much blood was everywhere on me and on my grandfather's shirt and he carried me in his arms into the house and he gave me to my mother as she was sitting in a chair and I cried and I cried but she would not hold me or kiss my wrists to make them better and instead she said,

"Be a big girl."

And she made me stand up and like that she walked me out of the house to the hospital like that without holding me and I had to get a tetanus shot and stitches and I didn't care anymore about my mother. I just didn't care.

❧ ❧ ❧

I had books and dolls and a dollhouse and a hammer and a fishing rod and a dog and puppies and a wagon and pencils and a pencil case, but I didn't have a gun.

I wanted a gun.

I never hankered after candy—or anything else, in fact, that I did not already possess.

Once I got a game that let you aim a ball into variously numbered landing areas, and I played with it endlessly until the launch spring gave out. But not having a game like that, neither before I got it nor after it broke, was perfectly fine with me.

I'd have to be standing two feet from the door to the subway nut shop, and I'd have to be about ready to swoon from the hot smell of roasted peanuts overtaking me, before my mother's query, "Would you like some cashew nuts?," made any sense to me.

If I thought she intended to buy them for me, I'd say, "Yes, thank you."

If I thought otherwise, I'd say, "No, thank you."

Either way, I'd mean what I said.

But I wanted a gun.

I asked for a gun.

I begged for a gun.

I worried about ways to get one on my own.

My mother refused to believe me.

She told me that little girls did not want guns.

Little girls wanted nice things, pretty things that would not hurt anybody.

The gun on my mind was a beautiful thing: Lean and clean and exactly what sleeping alone on the prairie seemed to require.

In the same way, I wanted a horse; and the horse had to be beautiful, too.

I wanted a horse.

But I knew there was "no room" for a horse in our house.

I had asked.

I wanted a gun.

And my father said I didn't need one. It would just be silly: A toy.

Or it would get me into trouble unless I learned how to use it.

And who would teach me?

He would not.

I didn't need one. I was living in Brooklyn. I was living at home with my parents. I didn't need one.

I wanted a gun.

I tried to think about how many things I ever wanted or asked for. I came up close to zero. So I felt gloomy.

I was only asking for one thing small enough for me to carry by myself.

And nobody would give it to me.

A gun was like a layaway toward a horse and a blanket-roll beside a fire under prairie stars.

A gun was useful in case of coyotes, rattlesnakes, cattle thieves, or other threatening outlaw personalities.

I wanted one.

⁂

It was hot and humid.

I was rolling marbles in the dirt. Now and then a mosquito distracted me. I'd smack my ear. I'd look around.

It was pretty quiet.

Was everybody else in the world asleep?

My Nanny called to me from the back porch. I should come upstairs and she'd wash me up and cool me down.

I ran inside and noticed that, underneath her apron, my Nanny was wearing an especially nice, an especially pretty dress.

It was gray with tiny white flowers sprinkled on top of that.

After pat-drying my face and hands with a washcloth, my

Nanny brushed my hair and tucked my tee shirt into my shorts.

She returned her apron to a kitchen hook, picked up her white patent-leather purse, her white cotton gloves, and, holding on to my hand, she left the house.

I loved going anywhere with my Nanny. Men and women went out of their way to say "Hello!" or "Afternoon, Mrs. Taylor!"

She'd just nod or answer them, "Fine. Fine," in a voice so hushed you couldn't make out the words, but nobody cared.

At the corner, we turned left. This meant we were heading into the white section of Central Avenue, the section with big stores and mostly white people on the sidewalk.

We kept going and I began to feel tired. We'd already passed the special treat playground that let you slide into grass and use trees as a jungle gym.

Nobody was saying "Hello!" anymore. But my Nanny stopped only for red lights, which she pointed out to me each time we paused at a corner.

At last she stood still in front of S. KRESGE / 5¢ AND 10¢.

"I'ma buy you a gun now, hmmph?!

"But you have to be telling me which one, hmmph?"

My heart was thumping thunder.

I followed my Nanny inside the store.

At the gun counter, I looked and I looked.

I could hardly think because my heartbeat was so loud.

My ears might burst.

My eyes searched for the biggest, the best, the most beautiful gun.

And I found it:

A .22 rifle with a really long blueblack barrel and a genuine wooden handle and a cylinder that flicked out so you could load and unload bullets easily.

So I picked it up. I pointed it at the floor and I pulled the trigger. And a cork popped out: A cork attached to a string inside the barrel of the gun.

It was just a toy.

I kept looking at the floor. I kept my eyes down there where the cork lay, silly and obvious to anyone who might pass by. I was afraid to say anything.

My Nanny was smiling at me.

She was hoping I was happy, and I was.

But not about the gun, which she bought for me, and which I carried by myself, and which I slept next to, and which I kept carrying by myself, outdoors and indoors, and even when I was supposed to be eating I carried my gun, my rifle, and I never let it slip from my sight because I had wanted a gun and my Nanny had bought me one and I knew I would never ever forget that.

part eight

MY UNCLE TEDDY, MY RACCOON, MY FIRST RESOLUTION

Besides my Nanny, there was somebody else: My Uncle Teddy.

Husband to Aunt Lynne, he was the first Black man of my life.

I adored him. It was mutual and it was deep. He called me Ace.

Long, long before I ever laid eyes on him, I learned from my father that my Uncle Teddy was "Black."

Again and again, my father derided my aunt: Why would she "t'row away" all "ambition," all "pride," and "mix up" herself with a "Black" man?!

For my benefit, my mother interjected that my Uncle Teddy was "an American, an American Negro."

This clarified nothing much.

I knew that my father regarded "American Negroes" as a completely different kind of people from West Indians.

He'd say that "they" suffered from an "inferiority complex," and that was why "they" let "the white man kick them around so."

He seemed to think that an "inferiority complex" was contagious.

He warned me not to "catch a complex" like that.

Upright posture and a lifted chin were two good ways to avoid sending a subservient signal to "the white man, them."

But on our block, American Negroes and West Indian families lived side by side, except that, as my father emphasized, no West Indians lived in the cold-water flats across the street.

But my father was enthusiastic and friendly with anybody he knew by name. And he knew the name of everybody on our block.

I decided that my Uncle Teddy must be dark-skinned. This made sense to me, since my aunt was dark-skinned.

I knew that my father was afraid of dark skin. Or he despised it.

I knew that anybody darker than my father became "Black," meaning low-down or despicable, if my father ever got angry.

Something about my Uncle Teddy really got on his nerves.

Aunt Lynne was my mother's baby sister, my mother's only blood relative besides my Nanny, who was also dark-skinned.

Aunt Lynne was Valerie's actual mother. But my parents had taken over for my aunt because she was always "getting an education."

This was a big habit of hers.

When my mother emigrated to America, she right away started working as a maid so that Aunt Lynne could finish up full-time at Hunter High School, where she graduated valedictorian.

Hunter High School was a special school in New York City. Not everyone could go there.

My aunt was "very smart."

But they didn't let her speak at the graduation. They said nobody could understand her West Indian "accent."

My mother said the problem was because the school was white.

After high school, my Aunt Lynne had to go to college, and after college she had to go to graduate school, and so my mother acquired her own big habit of supporting her baby sister's habit of "getting an education."

Once she got four or five academic degrees, my aunt also got pregnant. Then she gave birth to Valerie. But soon after Valerie was born, my aunt changed her mind about I'm not sure what, exactly, and the net result was that my parents raised Valerie, absent Aunt Lynne, for more than seven years.

That was why Valerie was living in the house with me.

During this time, somehow my Aunt Lynne met and married my Uncle Teddy, who was, however, far away in the United States Army, serving as a second lieutenant.

So, after she married him, and because he was far away, my aunt moved in with us.

My father ripped apart and then banged together and painted and polished the third floor of our house, and that became a "complete" apartment that he had created for my aunt. And that was where she was going to live in our house. And after she arrived, Valerie moved upstairs as well.

That Christmas, the mailman delivered an enormous package for Aunt Lynne.

It came from my Uncle Teddy. It was so heavy! My father helped her with it.

They rested it on the kitchen floor.

My mother produced a scissors.

My aunt cut it open.

Inside, a small white card said,

MERRY CHRISTMAS,

MADAME BUTTERFLY!

My aunt tittered like a girl.

I was completely fascinated!

What else would she find?

Setting aside the tissue paper, my aunt lifted out a long mink coat and struggled to stand up, still clasping it close.

My mother exclaimed, "A mink coat!"

My father kissed his teeth, and turned his back on the two women squealing with glee.

I had never heard of a mink coat. I had never seen a mink coat. But I got the definite impression that Uncle Teddy's present was something like a car.

It was not "a sacrifice."

I had never seen a present like that before! I had never heard of a present like that before!

I could hardly wait for my Uncle Teddy

to get out of the Army
and come home to my Aunt Lynne
and me!

⁂

Sure enough, my Uncle Teddy came to live with us when I was eight years old. And almost the first thing he did was buy a car.

It was a brand-new, rich blue Plymouth two-door sedan, with tan interior, whitewall tires, and deluxe chrome hubcaps.

I thought it was the most beautiful car in the world.

My father was completely disgusted.

But my Uncle Teddy's homecoming was unforgettable for several reasons.

He brought back two huge Army duffel bags and also a wooden Army trunk that was so big he and my father could barely get it through the front doors. And a raccoon.

The raccoon was a surprise for Ace.

That was *me.*

The wooden trunk was where the raccoon was supposed to stay, out in our backyard.

I had never seen a raccoon before. I couldn't believe that this wild animal was mine!

But it was: Even my father said so!

Immediately I planned how I would stroll up and down

Hancock Street, two or three times a day, with the raccoon on a leash attached to a puppy halter that would maybe have a bell on it.

Nobody knew what to feed it. I gave it chunks of iceberg lettuce, and whatever else I didn't particularly like to eat, from our refrigerator.

It was a really wild animal.

It was dangerous.

It was ready and eager to bite you.

I was pretty sure it would chew its way out of the wooden trunk.

But it was mine.

And I vowed I would take good care of it.

And I did.

And I tried to make friends with it.

I figured out how to hold it without getting bitten.

It was slow going.

And my excitement never dimmed.

Nobody could tell if it was a boy or a girl.

So I didn't give it a name besides My Raccoon.

It took me a couple days to accept that the black circles around its eyes didn't mean it was tired or sad.

I was very, very proud of My Raccoon.

I had a funny feeling on my way home from school.

When I rang the bell, it was my father who came to the gate, and he opened it without looking at me or saying anything.

But once I got past the front doors, he seized my arm so hard my eyes stung with tears.

> "Listen, now, you hear?
> You Raccoon him bite up you mother!
> An' she have go to the hospital
> an' she have come back
> from the hospital an' I gwine
> kill it now!"

He let go of my arm and he grabbed a broom and I knew he was going to beat My Raccoon to death and I screamed and I cried and he just shook me off and headed for the backyard.

And I was trembling and I couldn't make him hear me and I kept screaming and I kept crying and we got outside and he swung open the door of the Army trunk and he was trying to get My Raccoon to come out of its corner so he could beat it to death and I screamed and I cried and My Raccoon would not come out of its corner and then all of a sudden there was my Uncle Teddy and he snatched the broom out of my father's hand and said something like:

"Hey, Good Buddy!
Hey, Good Buddy!"
And then my Uncle Teddy said,
"Ace! Go and find your mother!
Go and bring your mother out here!"

So I ran to find my mother. And I found her. Her arm was bandaged up, but she was alive and everything. And I told my mother that my Uncle Teddy wanted her to come out to the backyard.

So she came out. And I could not stop trembling. I could not stop crying.

And my Uncle Teddy put his arm around me.

And everybody but me talked and talked.

And then my Uncle Teddy lifted me up into his arms and he walked around the yard with me.

And he told me My Raccoon was going to the zoo the very next day.

My Raccoon had to go there, he said.

But the zoo would take even better care of My Raccoon than I.

And I could visit it in the zoo.

Anytime, I could visit it there.

I didn't want to speak to my mother or my father.

I wanted to leave.

I didn't know where I could go.

So I sat at the kitchen table.

I tried not to be disrespectful.

I didn't want to fight anybody anymore.

※ ※ ※

I did visit My Raccoon at the Prospect Park Zoo.

But I couldn't tell which raccoon was mine.

And the cage seemed to me as high as the roof of my father's house.

So I thought My Raccoon might be happier there.

And safe.

※ ※ ※

I knew that if something hurt your girlfriend or your wife you were supposed to kill it.

I knew that.

But it had been an accident.

My Raccoon would not hurt my mother on purpose.

It had been an accident.

And what was she doing, anyway?

My Raccoon was mine: My

responsibility for food and exercise and cleaning up: mine.

It had been a bad accident.

An accident.

But I think my Uncle Teddy thought I was a boy. I could tell he didn't like girls. He paid no attention to Valerie. He ignored Valerie, except to tease her in a mean way.

He'd exaggerate the slew-footed way she walked. But he must have known she couldn't help that. And he'd order her around:

"You have fifteen minutes to clean the bathroom, starting. . . NOW!"

But he'd play with me. He'd come downstairs and he'd say, "'Tention!"

And I'd stand really erect and I'd hold my hand up at my forehead in a salute. And I'd stay like that until he said,

"At ease, Soldier!"

Then I'd adopt the correct "at ease" Army position he'd shown me.

And he coached me in boxing, too. But I never thought he'd knock me out. He always kept talking to me even as he feinted a left hook or a right-hand jab I needed to learn how to block.

My Uncle Teddy could talk and talk! I thought he could probably talk himself into heaven itself.

He had this rumbly, deep, deep voice, and in one sentence he might say something like:

"So I questioned the jurisprudence, the documented precedence for the court's prejudicial ruling, but I said to this rusty coon sitting up in the courtroom nasty as a skunk I said, Mista?! I so much as see your raggedy behind where it don't belong and I will personally make you wish yo' momma never had no babies! Do you understand me?!"

And my Uncle Teddy would snip the tip of another premium cigar, light a match, coddle the cigar until it lit, and then he'd laugh until his shoulders shook.

And I'd laugh too. And I'd pretend I couldn't remember the story so he'd say the whole thing all over again. So he would.

But he'd change the words each time, and it seemed to me he must know more words than the *Reader's Digest*!

And he would act out the parts of the story.

There would be the words he'd use "downtown," where white men "assumed" he was just "an ignorant cotton picker off the farm."

He'd beat them at their own vocabulary. And he'd demonstrate to me how he would appear to be concentrating on that Whiteman-Blackman conversation but, actually, he, my Uncle Teddy, would be studying his shoes and gloating over the five-dollar shine he'd given them himself.

Or he'd dramatize how he "ran down" this "sorry excuse for a Negro" in a bar and grill and how he explained to him that he'd "pistol-whip his kinky handkerchief-square head from here to kingdom come" if he, my Uncle Teddy, ever had to spend time looking like that again for "garbage just don't know how loud it smells."

⁂ ⁂ ⁂

Even though he'd graduated from law school, my Uncle Teddy said he would never "practice law" because "the whiteman's not about to let a well-dressed, sweet-talking Negro sit up in some office just like he's a regular man."

He was a parole officer. My Aunt Lynne was a math teacher. My mother often said they had "education in common."

⁂ ⁂ ⁂

But my Uncle Teddy talked so good! He could have been the ugliest, ugliest man in the neighborhood and it would have been obvious why anyone would marry him.

He'd talk her into it.

He could make anything happen with words.

He could rile my father with a single word: He'd call my father Granny!

And they'd fight. But it was pretty even.

My father would get my uncle down on the ground.

Or my Uncle Teddy would pin my father to the wall.

I thought they had a lot "in common."

Both of them loved clothes. But my father would show me how to use saddle soap to preserve shoes, and my Uncle Teddy would show me how to make shoes shine.

They both fancied expensive suits and overcoats.

But my father would lie down in his Sunday suit, listening to classical music in the parlor.

And I knew my Uncle Teddy would never risk that kind of rumpling up.

He'd sit with his legs crossed, relishing the dry-cleaner crease of his trousers and the thin dress socks that perfectly matched his silk tie.

But I never saw my father cross his legs.

They both spent a lot of time in front of the mirror: Shaving and grooming their hair.

They both married beautiful women.

But my Aunt Lynne wore high heels all the time and my mother alternated between nurse's shoes and broken-down Hush Puppies.

They both ridiculed whatever women friends my mother and/or my Aunt Lynne might invite into the house.

They'd both summarize those female get-togethers as "yakkety-yak-yak yakkety-yak-yak" sessions of no merit: A waste of time!

They both insisted on major-production cooking rights.

My father composed gargantuan pots of rice and peas that even he could not move off the stove.

My Uncle Teddy prepared battalion-size quantities of chitlins and pigs' feet and pepper-hot potato salad to garnish his weekly pinochle games that went on, uproarious, until dawn, while he and his friends downed amazing amounts of bourbon and scotch and ginger ale chasers as they smoked limitless numbers of cigars and cigarettes.

At the end, my Uncle Teddy would break out a gallon of ice cream that some parolee had wistfully stolen for him: A poor man's effort at lightening the lash.

I'd race up the stairs and try to see and taste everything at once.

My Uncle Teddy would put me on his lap and show me his cards. He'd say, "Ace? What do you think I should do next?"

And I'd just smile because I was happy. And he'd say,

"Uh-huh! I'll do it!"

And all the men would laugh, and my Uncle Teddy would slap down his cards on the table and say, like a second lieutenant,

"Ex-cuse me!"

And he'd get up and take me into the kitchen and fix a paper plate for me that included the ice cream right beside the pigs' feet and he'd say,

"Now! If I were you,
I'd finish off that ice cream
right away! Before
it melts!
And then I'd bump my gums on some pigs' feet
make my eyes roll around in my head
and my tongue hang out—"

At which point my Aunt Lynne might primly interrupt:

"Teddy. . . ."

⁂

My Uncle Teddy's full name was Theodore Roosevelt Rutledge, which sounded to me a lot like Granville Ivanhoe Jordan.

But they were not twins.

Rather than having a good time, my father devoted himself only to things that were "good for you": Things that "built character" or "sharpened up your mind" or "put hair on your chest."

He'd say, "Eat up the spinach!
An' put hair on your chest!"
And I'd say, "No, thank you, Daddy!"
And he'd say, "But, what?!
You don' wan' hair grow

an' fill out your chest?"
And I'd say, "No, thank you, Daddy!"
And sometimes he'd insist on the spinach.
And sometimes I'd resist.
And those times I'd get a beating.

⁂

My Uncle Teddy loved to sing and he loved to play blues piano.

He and his brother, Uncle Eddy, would drink and smoke and wear suspenders, and they'd duet at the piano and they'd take turns singing or punching out a song on the keys, and hours would go by and I had never seen anything like it.

Even when my Uncle Teddy simonized the Plymouth parked out front, he sang. Shining his shoes, he sang.

And he could sing good as he could talk—his voice rippled from a blues baritone to a soulful-shack falsetto.

He and Uncle Eddie would make that music jump and swing, and they did all of that by ear, just horsing around:

"Oh! I went down to the St. James Infirmary
(bump, bump)
To see my ba-bee there!
(bump)..."

Luckily for me, they fooled around like this almost any Friday night.

And I'd sit on my father's fully restored hard-back Victorian couch and I'd try to memorize every detail, down to the color and the tension of my Uncle Teddy's suspenders.

But it wasn't just the good times that mattered so much.

More than once, when my father cornered me and lost control and looked like he wanted to kill me, my Uncle Teddy intervened: He'd just grab my father's fist or wrap his arm around my father's throat, and he'd say,

"Pick on a man your own size!"

That's what he'd always say.

And when my mother pushed aside my report card and changed the subject, my Uncle Teddy would retrieve it and seem to study it, and then he'd say,

"Ace!"

And I'd answer him, "Yes, Uncle Teddy?"

And he'd say,

"You know what I am?"

And I'd say, "No, Sir."

And he'd say,

"I'm proud of you!

I'm proud of you!"

❧❧❧

And then there was Daisy Mae Johnson. She hated me. And I was afraid of her. And I didn't know why.

So Daisy Mae made me walk up the school stairs two steps behind her.

Or she made me throw out my lunch.

And she'd tell me I better not use this or that door to leave school.

And I was scared.

I did whatever she told me to.

But somehow my mother found out about it. And she told my Uncle Teddy.

And he came home early from work and drove me and my mother to Daisy Mae Johnson's house.

I absolutely did not want to go.

And worse than my mother having found out was my Uncle Teddy:

He must be ashamed of me.

I just wanted to die.

But we got to Daisy Mae Johnson's house.

Her mother acted like a nice lady.

She called to Daisy Mae and Daisy Mae came into the living room where we were, and she sat down.

And my Uncle Teddy let everything get real quiet.

Then he said, "Ace? Is that Daisy Mae?"

And I answered him, "Yes, Sir."

And he said, "Ace?

Is that little girl, just a little bit bigger, just a little bit older than you are, who is sitting down just like you, and whose mother is in the room just like your mother—is that little girl Daisy Mae Johnson?"

And I answered him, "Yes, Sir."

Then my Uncle Teddy said,

"Ace? What are you afraid of?!"

And I looked over at Daisy Mae and then I looked back at my Uncle Teddy, and I said, "Nothing, Sir."

Then my Uncle Teddy laughed and he said,

"I didn't think so! Not my Ace!"

And he suggested that Daisy Mae and I shake hands.

So we stood up and we did.

Then my mother and my Uncle Teddy and I left Daisy Mae Johnson's house.

On the sidewalk, my Uncle Teddy held me by my shoulders and said,

"Ace! Look me in the eye!"

So I lifted my chin up to look him in the eye.

"What are you afraid of?"

And I answered him, "Nothing, Sir."

And my Uncle Teddy laughed and said,

"Now, that's what I'm talking about! That's *my* Ace!"

And at that moment I felt like I was making myself a promise: A big one.

part nine

BRAVERY, HEROES, AND SOME COMPLICATIONS

My father thought very highly of Marcus Garvey, but to me Marcus Garvey was dead.

All my heroes turned out to be American Negroes. For example, there was Mr. Epps.

As soon as he left the Army, he opened up a laundromat on the corner of Hancock Street and Reid Avenue: That was at the end of our block!

Just past the Holy Tabernacle storefront you could watch through the mail slot if you lay down on your belly, just past that tabernacle of tambourines and foot-stomps and shouts to Lord Jesus, Mr. Epps established the first Negro-owned family business in our neighborhood.

It was also the first laundromat. And my Nanny traveled from New Jersey to inspect and verify this wonder for herself.

She and my mother and I made a stately beeline to that miracle we needed to behold together.

And, yes, there was Mr. Epps!

He seemed quite happy to welcome us. He guided us around the pristine premises.

There must have been twenty machines, side by side.

And we stared at the four mammoth "dryers" in silence.

My Nanny and my mother couldn't imagine an appropriate question, even, and so they just stood there smiling.

Embarassed by their silence, Mr. Epps asked if they'd like to see the machines in motion.

And he threw some demonstration rags and soap powder into a machine.

And we watched as bubbly soap water rose behind the machine's porthole, and we could hear as well as eyewitness the rhythmical churning of "the wash cycle."

Next came "Rinse." Then "Spin."

Mr. Epps removed the clean, wrung rags and offered them to my Nanny and my mother.

But both of them backed away.

So he threw the rags into "the dryer," and after that processing he removed them and again offered this fresh evidence for their examination.

Again both of them backed away, and in fact both my Nanny and my mother more or less backed all the way out of that laundromat until they found themselves safely outside.

⁂ ⁂ ⁂

But Joe Louis was the one!

Before I could steady run around on my own two feet, I heard about him.

"Joe! C'mon Joe! C'mon Joe!"

He made everybody laugh and clap and hug me, too.

Joe was better than Jesus.

You couldn't see him, but he just about came through the radio.

Joe was always fighting, and he knew how.

Mostly, he'd win.

But even if he lost, my father slammed doors and yelled, "That's okay, now! He coming back!"

He belonged to us.

He was the Brown Bomber.

He beat the Nazis.

He was Heavyweight Champion of the World!

And he was ours.

I think he only used to fight before it was my bedtime.

I got to listen to it once we moved to Brooklyn.

It would be the biggest happening!

"The fight's tonight! The fight's tonight!"

And my mother organized. She pulled a chair to the sink and chose a pot she could easily handle.

She lined up towels and shampoo and me.

She timed this ritual so that, when at last somebody started to sing "The Star-Spangled Banner," I'd no longer be kneeling on the chair and hanging my head under the sink faucet while she soaped and rinsed my hair.

No! Just as the national anthem began, I'd be sure enough seated on a low stool between her knees while she settled into the untangling and the oiling and the braiding of my "tender-headed" hair.

Looking at the off-kilter and rhapsodic expression on her

face, I'd think it was just as well she didn't need to concentrate on what she was doing.

But, suffering the yanks and the determined, erratic tugs of the big-tooth comb she jammed into my hair and then absent-mindedly extricated at disagreeably unpredictable moments, I'd wish she'd concentrate a little bit nevertheless.

The referee, the contender for the crown, the champion, the sportscasters, the astonishing rapid-fire verbal descriptions, my mother's tension, my mother's palpable jubilation, my aching scalp, the general wailing or hallelujah salute to Joe's "solid right to the heart" of his opponent entirely, entirely intoxicated me.

I thought, "This is the way to fight! This is the way to win!"

I couldn't see how you could lose with my mother rooting for you.

How could you lose if the whole block wanted you to win?

My father said Joe was "clean." He lived "clean." He fought "clean."

With my own ears I heard Joe Louis thank God, everybody, and his mother at the end of every bout.

My father said Joe Louis was "a humble man."

I just loved Joe Louis.

He didn't show off. He only fought people his own size.

He only "defended" himself, "defended" his crown.

But when he left his corner of the ring when the bell rang for Round One, Joe Louis charged out to meet his man.

He practiced.

He trained.

He didn't talk much.

He was a winner.

And then he'd do that thank-you thing, which I found very interesting.

He must know we wanted him to win. He must know God wanted him to win.

And that must have helped him somehow.

But how did he know that?

How?

How could you tell?

⁂

To me, Joe Louis was like the Bible, except Joe Louis was alive.

And fighting was a really good way to live.

There was nothing wrong about it.

Joe Louis made that obvious.

⁂

Besides Joe Louis, I could never get enough of thunderstorms, snow, and church.

Snow changed everything. Even the soft start of the falling snowflakes filled me with wonder and hope.

Perhaps it would never stop. Perhaps the snow would thicken and cling to the intricate outdoor iron railings and the concrete curbstone and the stripped-down tree limbs and my nose.

Schools might close!

Perhaps the ground would crunch and let me track the footsteps of strangers. Perhaps huge mounds of snow would block all cars and I could race and belly-whop on wooden sleds as straightaway as you could steer.

And I always expected something else.

And I never knew what.

* * *

But church was the only reliable excitement. It was completely different, but regular.

* * *

Thunderstorms took you by surprise: Boom! Bang! Crack! It was happening.

I'd feel so suddenly connected to the sky itself: Almost, almost pierced by its sound, commanding me to wait, to listen for more, for whatever next might clarify the world.

And then the lightning: So exquisitely precise and bright and brief!

And then the holy water of that rainy aftermath that pearled and pooled against all hardness of the earth.

⁂

Dr. Clement E. Davis said he wasn't sure I'd live to be ten years old.

I was eight.

He was serious.

My mother shook her head and looked at me.

He'd never seen such a "tomboy."

He'd never known such an "accident-prone" little girl.

If only I'd "cut out the rough stuff and behave" myself, I might make it.

Otherwise?

He shook his head.

I sat on the edge of the examining table, minus one shoe and one sock.

They said I had something called a "planter's wart" embedded in the sole of my right foot.

Dr. Davis was going to use a knife to remove it. Then he was going to "cauterize the area." And then he was going to apply "acid" so the plantar wart would not return.

We were waiting for the local anesthesia to take effect.

I didn't like Dr. Davis as much as my mother did.

She seemed to think he was very handsome.

Usually they laughed a lot while I sat around. Usually he was supposed to fix something of mine: A fractured rib, a broken arm, a "baseball finger."

Once in a while he'd come to our house if my asthma got very bad, and still he and my mother would laugh a lot.

And when we went to his office we'd have to spend three or four hours in his overcrowded waiting room. But each time, my mother would remind me that Dr. Davis was a West Indian doctor, from Jamaica.

She meant me to understand that just seeing a Jamaican doctor was worth it.

I did not agree.

But my mother never asked me.

And now our waiting on the local anesthesia was over.

As requested, I lay down on the table, and Dr. Davis began to operate on my foot.

He was humming and singing a comical Calypso melody as he proceeded.

But I could hardly breathe!

The pain left me breathless, speechless.

I blinked and blinked.

"It hurts!," I managed to say.

Dr. Davis seemed annoyed! To my mother he explained that there must not have been enough anesthesia; the wart was way deeper than he had estimated; he couldn't interrupt, however, because the wound was wide open; he needed to finish the surgery, and the rest of it, without anesthesia for me.

Sweat poured from my head.

I bit through my lower lip, determined not to cry.

My mother's face appeared above mine.

She looked gentle.

She looked like she felt sorry for me.

She murmured something about "Be a big girl; try!"

Dr. Davis teased me: "Be a big boy! C'mon now! Boys don't cry!"

I was not crying.

I was having trouble breathing.

Every jab or swerve of the knife jabbed and swerved inside my head, which throbbed and felt like it was bulging.

But I was not crying.

My mother held me down by my shoulders.

But I was not moving.

I was engulfed and stabbed by and scraped by a ferocious agony I could not begin to describe to myself.

Then it stopped.

Dr. Davis held up a long, wormy-looking thing and said that was the root of the wart and, as I could see, it was really long, which was to say really deep and hideous, but now, as I could see, it was out of my foot, out of me.

I looked.

But Dr. Davis had not finished. He still needed "to cauterize" the area and apply the "acid."

He told me that it would burn.

He switched on a motor and my foot began to burn.

He was burning my foot!

I couldn't help it anymore.

Tears came out of my eyes.

And then he finished.

He bandaged my foot. He said I'd been very brave.

I didn't care what he thought about me.

I hated him, and I hated my mother, too.

I didn't want to stay there.

And I didn't want to go home.

Pocket money was always a problem. I needed some. But my parents didn't think so.

And I could never explain that it was never about candy.

I had to invent a little bit of independent income by myself.

And I did.

I converted the wooden wagon my father had given to me after he'd painted it red with a lime green interior—I converted that into a business.

Starting with my parents' house, I went door-to-door, collecting bottles.

Some weeks the refund on my neighborhood haul amounted to two or three dollars.

I could hardly believe how fast the nickels added up!

But the business was subject to the weather.

It was seasonal at best.

I needed an alternative, weatherproof supplement of cash.

Poetry became that reliable, if meager, mainstay.

Rhyming amused me for hours. And as matter of fact, even when no one else found it amusing, I found that hilarious, too.

I was pretty silly:

"Hi! Bye! See you tomorrow! Sigh!"

"You'll feel better if you wear a sweater!"

And so forth.

But there had been a poetry contest in school for Flag Day.

And I'd been utterly dumbfounded.

Did the teacher want a poem about the flag, or about the day the flag was born, or about flying the flag, or what?

I just wrote about the colors and the stars and the song about whether you could see them or not.

And I won.

This dumbfounded me as well.

Why did I win?

What did everyone else write about?

How could I win a contest centered on something I didn't really care about or understand?

In the poetry my father made me memorize, there was always somebody involved, somebody obvious as the reason for the poem.

None of them seemed to be only about a *thing,* like the flag.

School was bewildering, for sure.

But one thing I got out of it: I was a winner!

I was a winner at poetry.

I thought I should try and make something out of that. Like, for example, money.

So I tried.

I offered to compose poetry for my friends in need of an "I Like You" or "I Don't Like You" or "I Don't Like You Anymore" poem.

And depending on the length, and depending on how hard it was for me to figure out what really was the purpose of the poem, I charged anywhere from ten cents to twenty-five.

This was not much money.

But occasionally I might earn as much as an extra dollar for a month's work.

I liked the whole process.

I liked having something I could do that other people might ask me for.

I liked finding out about feelings or secret wishes besides my own.

And then I liked matching up words with those feelings.

I liked that a lot.

❧ ❧ ❧

But free time was pretty scarce. I developed a way of dreaming all of the time, no matter what.

I could even talk or listen and keep on dreaming.

It wasn't so much a dream about anything.

It was more like staring at a stain on my mother's apron and then not forgetting that stain as I walked to school or went out to play.

Or the hairs inside my father's ear.

Or the smell of my new notebook.

Or the darkness at the top of the stairs leading to my room.

❧ ❧ ❧

More often than I was happy about, my mother had me "fitted" for yet another "special dress."

This meant standing perfectly still while Mrs. De Freitas, a neighbor lady who lived three houses away, measured me and fidgeted around my knees with bunches of straight pins stuck between her lips.

I mainly kept still because I didn't want Mrs. De Freitas to swallow the pins.

Maybe the fittings happened only two or three times.

But I dreaded them.

My mother seemed so intent upon every detail: The cost of the material, the fullness of the sleeves, the width of the sash!

Mrs. De Freitas crouched close to my ankles as she experimented with this or that.

It made me uncomfortable for a grown-up to be hovering so far below my head.

They kept jotting down numbers and fractions on a little white pad.

Then they'd erase them and start over.

These fittings took place in a corner of Mrs. De Freitas's bedroom.

It was not easy to stand or turn in that small, jammed-up space.

I worried that nothing good enough would come of all that fuss; nothing good enough to let my mother and Mrs. De Freitas sit back, satisfied.

* * *

And I sang at the top of my lungs! I sang so loud! Everybody on the block could hear me! I sang so loud!

I'd rush out to the backyard, and I'd sing with all my might!

I'd sing until my ears hurt. I'd sing and sing until I ran out of the words for a song.

Then I'd stop, but only then.

I think that was why my parents decided I should take singing lessons.

They wanted me to learn how to sing *inside* the house.

They wanted me to learn how to sing like a girl.

So I learned.

But I never gave up the other way, my other way of singing.

I was already taking piano lessons, which was okay.

For me, playing the piano was very much like boys:

I didn't have to prove anything.

Valerie played the piano so well!

I could just play.

And I even liked practicing my scales.

I liked using my eyes and my ears, arms, wrists, hands, and fingers for something that, in the end, was so different from any of those!

In the end, there was music: I was making music!

It was fun!

But the actual lessons bothered me. There was no choice about them.

My music teacher, Mrs. Edwards, lived in a shadowy, large place with framed photographs and dusty air and the old slippers and the worn pyjamas of her deceased husband, Bunny.

She missed Bunny.

She intended to keep "his things out, forever," or until she died too.

It felt creepy to me.

She was always chewing a last bit of cake or speaking in a very soft voice, except when she'd rap my knuckles with a heavy lead pencil.

She'd say, "You know, he was my great, great love. . . ."

And I'd look around.

And I'd see so many shadows everywhere.

⁂

Being cool was a matter of style. But being brave was a matter of virtue.

I wanted to be brave. It was something I thought about and worked on.

From my father and from everything I read, I got the impression that bravery was the only way to save your life, or the life of somebody else.

It seemed clear that serious danger, of one kind or another, was generally lurking pretty close by.

In the stories, it would be a lion's den or jealous brothers or a battlefield or a river flooding its banks.

There was not much I heard about that matched up with Brooklyn or my family.

But I knew fear. Frequently I felt afraid. And whenever I recognized that feeling, I set out to test myself and move ahead.

So I tested myself all the time.

It was a point of honor.

⁂

People used to say I was a brave little girl or that I was brave like a boy—a lot.

My street reputation for "crazy" was just one version of this.

My mother seemed to believe I was "fearless."

And I couldn't tell if she was glad about that or just matter-of-fact.

But I knew she assumed that was true.

⁂

One weekend this lady named Aunt Albee came to our house to die.

She had never visited before.

She seemed old, but I was not sure how old.

My mother acted like there was nothing peculiar underway.

I don't remember if Aunt Albee ate anything before she went upstairs to the parlor, lay down on a couch, and died.

But, anyway, she died—lying on her back. And after a while my mother came into the kitchen and told me Aunt Albee was dead.

There was a big pause because I couldn't even think of anything to say.

Then my mother said she needed me to help and she knew I could help her because I was like a little doctor: I was not afraid of anything.

I thought to myself, *Uh-oh; What's about to happen?* I kept quiet. I followed my mother back to the parlor.

She opened the door and indicated I should precede her into the room.

I stood in the middle of the rug and peered over at Aunt Albee.

She was not making any noise.

My mother beckoned me to come closer, and I did.

I stood right beside that lady. My mother repeated, "Aunt Albee is dead."

And then she said she was going to fold Aunt Albee's arms over Aunt Albee's chest, and that while she was doing that I should reach up and shut Aunt Albee's eyelids, which, until my mother mentioned them, I had not noticed: They seemed to be stuck open.

I stalled.

I did not want to touch this strange lady.
I did not want to touch anybody dead.
And what if her eyelids were really stuck open?
How was I supposed to make them close?
I did not move.
My mother asked me, "What is the matter?"
And I thought she was about to add on,
"Are you afraid?"
And so I reached out and put my index
finger on Aunt Albee's left eyelid, and
closed it, and then I used the same
finger to shut the other eyelid,
and then I wanted to cut off
that finger: My own finger.
I wanted nothing to do with the dead.

Not long after this, my mother worried about bowel movements every morning. She'd ask if I'd had one. She'd say she'd had one or she hadn't.

This was every morning. It was more casual than changing the station on the radio: Did you move your bowels?

Soon there appeared a large blue-and-white bottle of Phillip's Milk of Magnesia. It stood on the kitchen table next to the jars of marmalade and honey and Worcestershire sauce.

Then my mother began "to give" herself "enemas."

All of this bowel movement stuff was making me sick.

Because the bathroom was actually a walled-off part of the kitchen, there was no escape.

Either she'd be taking something in order to have a bowel movement or she'd be having or not having one and, in any case, it was all happening or not happening in the same space.

I felt trapped.

* * *

I was doing my homework. My mother had gone into the bathroom and she had not come out.

And then she called to me.

I pretended not to hear.

But she called to me again.

So I answered her, "Yes, mommy?"

And she asked me to come inside the bathroom.

I put down my pencil.

I looked at the clock above the refrigerator.

I looked at the bars behind the broad kitchen window.

I looked at the open pages of my book.

I pushed back my chair and stood up.

I went to the bathroom door and opened it.
My mother had hitched up her dress to her waist.
There was an enema bag lying in the sink.
She was sniffling and crying and speaking to me.
She was half-naked.
She needed to have a bowel movement, but
she could not do that by herself.
She needed my help.
"The stool" was too hard.
It wouldn't come out.
She needed me for that.
She knew it was a lot to ask.
But she also knew how brave I was.
So she was asking me.
"Help me!," she said.
I felt as stiff as heavy as lead.
Minutes went by.
I stood still.

In my mind there was a question I was fighting against as best I could, but the question kept circling back to my mouth and finally I asked my mother,

"You want me to use my hand?"
She nodded her head and I could see she was crying.

"I'll guide you," she said.

And she did.

And afterward she scrubbed my fingertips with a brush and she washed and washed my hand and she thanked me, again and again.

And I left her alone in the bathroom. I stood outside that door.

I looked at my hand.

I walked over to my homework.

I looked at my pencil lying there.

I looked down at my hand.

I left the house.

I wanted to cry.

But I couldn't do it.

I could not.

part ten

PROMISES, APPLE TREES, AND PRETTY MISS KITTY

I didn't know too much about promises. But I knew it was dishonorable to break them.

My father promised me a regular two-wheel bicycle with thin tires if I got straight *A*s on my final report cards for two semesters in a row.

This made me mad.

I always got good grades. I wanted a bicycle. I couldn't see what one thing should have to do with the other.

But what was worse was when I got all *A*s and still I didn't get a bicycle.

I didn't want to listen to him anymore. I wanted a bicycle.

Then my father promised he would get me a bicycle if I got straight *A*s one more time.

So I brought my next report card home.

Every grade was A or A+.

Then my father said,

"See what you do now?! If you put you mind to it, heh?"

And he lectured me about the value of school versus the "triflin'" value of a bicycle, and I saw where he was heading but I couldn't do anything to turn him around.

He wanted me to prove I really really cared about school. I'd prove *that* if I got straight *A*s just one more time again.

Then straight *A*s would become "a second nature" to me, and then it would be all right for me to have a bicycle, because by then I'd realize that a bicycle was not "the end-all and be-all" of life.

I could hardly look at him, my father, while he talked to me.

I was not getting a bicycle.

He was breaking his promise.

He had broken his promises.

I wondered what was it about a bicycle! Why couldn't I have one?

That semester ended, and again I earned straight *A*s, but I didn't say anything about my grades or the bicycle.

I was through with the whole thing.

But a few days later an enormous box arrived. It was my bicycle!

It was my brand-new bicycle!

But it was packed inside this big box and somebody would have to pry open the box and then assemble the parts.

My father did not have the time.

My mother did not know how.

I couldn't stand it.

So I hacked at the cardboard and I

pulled the parts out and then I stared

at the gleaming mess of bicycle

machinery heaped on the ground.

I couldn't stand it.

So I looked at the instructions and then I threw them away

and I assembled my bicycle myself and I tightened the screws and I fooled with the handlebars and I lowered the seat spike into place and I didn't stop to take an overall look at my bicycle because I was so excited I took it outside and I got on my new bicycle and I started to laugh and I was riding my brand-new bike on Hancock Street and because the tires were thin I was flying along and when I got to the corner I leaned way to the right and I was laughing still and pedaling like this was the way I was supposed to fly around and then this Cadillac driven by a white man hit my new bicycle and I went flying off my bicycle and I didn't land okay so I "sustained a concussion" and when I regained my consciousness it was a hospital bed that I was lying in and there was no sign of my bicycle anywhere and I started to wonder again about the problem about me and a bicycle but then I remembered I had put my bike together by myself and so I thought maybe I could fix it by myself when I got out of there.

But I didn't listen to what anybody
said about when I'd be able to leave the hospital.
I knew better.

⁂

But I want to remember the roses! In my father's garden, red ones, white ones, tangerine, and pink: Some of them grew on their own, scraggly and not so pretty as they might hope to be unless you sniffed into the pollen-powder heart of every rose and you forgot about the crooked stem the thorns the sometime bees the not so nice not regular see-through of the edgy leaves then, then!—it could become so sweet a thing a rose just standing by itself.

Or if they got to be a bush of roses or a lifted climb along a trellis that became invisible behind that beautiful slow move to spread and reach and swell before the petals fell and falling lost the bloom the smell of roses anybody still alive could recognize as roses then, then!—that could be so sweet a thing a thrill of roses generous as air.

⁂

I knew I was not an apple. But I was sure trying to hang up there in the centerpiece apple tree of Brooklyn's YWCA Robin Hood Camp for Girls, in Central Valley, New York.

I was nine years old. I was two and a half hours by bus away from Hancock Street. And I had stuck myself up in an apple tree because now I was free. I was free! Nobody knew how to make me come down.

I couldn't get over it!

The camp director, my counselor, my bunkmates—all gave it a shot.

They stood under the apple tree, one way or another,

telling me it was time to quit. I should jump, or whatever, back to the ground and be done with it.

The grown-ups reasoned with me. Why not abandon the tree? What about lunch? Wasn't I hungry? Wouldn't I feel cold that night, out there by myself?

If I came down, there would be no hard feelings, no punishment, but "Jump!"

I was pretty high, wedged in the branches near the very top, and I was pretty comfortable, and I was not about to jump.

Climbing up had seemed easy to me, a lot easier than the prospect of climbing down.

To tell the truth, I couldn't figure out how I'd get out of the tree, exactly.

I needed time to think it through. Meanwhile, the other campers appeared and disappeared, giggling and teasing and making up horror stories.

I had no idea what to do.

It was my third week at camp. It was my first time away from home or family.

About a month before I left, my Nanny had come to our house and stayed several days.

My mother had purchased every item of clothing on the SUGGESTED LIST for campers and then every single tee shirt and every single sock had to have my name sewn into it. So my

Nanny and my mother sewed and sewed my name, and my Nanny used a thimble, which I thought looked like jewelry on her fingertip, but I watched them sewing without stop and I wondered if one or both of them would become permanently blind just because I was going away to camp, which was not anything either my Nanny or my mother knew anything about.

I didn't think that would be fair.

But neither my Nanny nor my mother would skip a stitch or stuff one named sock inside a matching unnamed sock. All of it had to be done, and done right.

I was going to camp.
My father had announced that as a fact.
It would be good for me.
I would learn "how to handle myself."
And, for our information, the rich
people's children ("*them*") did not stay
on the street "running wild"
in the summertime.
No!
They went away to camp.
And so would I.
That was as much as I knew.

⁂

On the morning of my departure, my mother cried. My father fumed. And I refused to eat my breakfast.

In front of the downtown YWCA, three buses pulled up. There were parents and children and suitcases and boxes for sending dirty laundry home—all of these were scrambled together on the sidewalk.

I noticed that everybody around my size seemed to be a girl. I noticed that everybody besides my parents and me seemed to be white people.

But more than anything else, I noticed a lot of hugging and kissing and I wondered about that.

When it was time, I boarded the bus as I was told and took my seat.

I looked through my windowpane at the grown-ups left behind. They looked small. My mother and my father looked small and short. I knew they were my parents. And I didn't know who they were.

I wondered if I would ever see them again.

When the white lady told us to give "a big smile and a big wave to your folks," I waved at them.

My mother just stood there, and I noticed that one of her shoulders was drooping.

I had never noticed that before.

My father gave me a right-handed military salute.

We were on our way.

* * *

Robin Hood Camp was country. It was beautiful. It was full of other girls my age or older. And nobody's mother or father was allowed to come there except on Visiting Sundays.

When I saw the daily mimeographed schedule and I heard the rules, I thought the Army must be exactly like Robin Hood, except we were only supposed to be playing:

7:00 A.M.	*Wake-Up Bugle Call*
7:15 A.M.	*Washhouse*
7:30–8:30 A.M.	*Breakfast*
8:45–9:15 A.M.	*Make Beds / Clean Up: Cabin Inspection*
9:20–9:50 A.M.	*Arts and Crafts*
10:00–11:00 A.M.	*Swimming (Instruction)*
11:15–12:00 P.M.	*Library / Free Time*
12:15 P.M.	*Lunch*
1:15 P.M.	*Rest Hour (including once-a-week letter to your parents)*

2:15 P.M.	*Boating*
	or
	Camp Craft
3:30 P.M.	*Softball*
	or
	Volleyball
	or
	Archery
5:00 P.M.	*Swimming (No Instruction)*
	or
	Tennis (Instruction)
6:15 P.M.	*Dinner*
7:30 P.M.	*Music or Stories or Skits*
	in the Rec. Hall
	or
	Campfire
8:30 P.M.	*Washhouse*
9:00 P.M.	*Cabin Call*
9:30 P.M.	*"Taps" by Bugle*
LIGHTS OUT	

One really terrific thing about Robin Hood Camp was that there were no lights. Other than in a few of the common areas, there was no electricity.

Counselors patrolled the paths with lanterns that curved their swinging yellow light into the darkness.

The washhouse offered cold running water and a john that was actually a long outhouse partitioned into stalls with wooden gates rather than doors.

I heard about copperhead snakes and bats and poison ivy before I dozed off my first night.

There was so much whispering after dark! There was so much cricket-throbbing all around us!

We slept six or eight cots to a cabin. The cabins were half wood and half screen.

Somebody would ask: "Are you scared?"

And no one would ever say yes.

I got the impression that we were supposed to be scared but never admit it.

But for me that was a strange possibility: For the first time in my life I was not sleeping alone; I could hear the girl beside me turn in her sleep or change the rhythm of her breathing. What could surprise or scare me here?

But I was not prepared for dawn.

Very carefully I opened my eyes and looked to my left and my right: Everybody was sleeping. I felt cold but I did not stir. I could see something shift and lighten through the screens.

It was the sky.

It kept shifting the darkness aside. It kept lightening the space around our cabin. I couldn't think of a word for the coloring of what was making my heart beat so fast.

I lay there so happy.

Maybe this was why they sewed my name on everything.

Otherwise I might forget it.

Otherwise I might want to forget my name.

⁂

Permissible variations on our days included horseback riding and—if you'd proven your campcraft mettle—overnight or even three-day hiking trips into the mountains.

There was not much time to feel lonely.

Even when it rained, you could still do almost everything except play ball, which I was one thousand percent enthusiastic about: Any kind of ball!

Even after "Taps" you could still read by flashlight under the blanket.

I thought camp was the best!

I could not stop laughing!

I ran to every activity! I ran down the steep rocky dirt to the lake! I ran up the hill to the dining hall.

I could not stop running!

I thought that Wednesday's "chow mein" was the most delicious dinner and I tried for thirds and fourths.

I had always loved the story of Robin Hood. I had always thought he could see straight, could ride straight-arrow through the woods, and I would've joined him in a minute!

And now I was falling in love with a world named after him.

Because of Robin Hood I was falling in love with the world.

⁂

Pretty soon it was clear that everybody at camp was not a girl.

Girls threw the ball funny.

Girls complained about bugs.

Girls got tired.

Girls hated the cold lake water.

Girls got homesick.

Girls could never keep score.

Girls discovered somebody had shorted their sheets so they couldn't get into bed.

Girls found salamanders in their shoes.

Girls collapsed in their cots that we rigged so that they would—collapse.

A girl was probably not a good camper.

For sure, a girl was probably not having a very good time at camp.

It's not that the rest of us were boys. But we were not "girls," either.

We were "Cabin Four!" or "Team B!" or a motley gamut of cartoon nicknames.

For example, my best friend was Judith Oliver. And mostly we called her Jodi. And that was fine. But she wore a rabbit's foot around her neck. So for a while some of us tried calling her Rabbit or Rabbit Foot. But it never went anywhere.

She was just Jodi. She had tiger eyes and a lion's mane for hair and she chewed gum so that it cracked near her chipped front tooth and her skin turned the same color as my own skin from the sun and I always thought she must really be an Indian because she was so graceful and tough and strong and she could walk on leaves and you wouldn't hear her coming and she could ride a horse English saddle like it was a Western saddle and the best thing was that Jodi was bowlegged.

I thought she was so lucky! I did everything I could dream up to be bowlegged, too, but nothing worked.

The most I could manage was a pretend-bowlegged way of standing around.

But anyway Jodi was my best friend: In fact she was the first girl I thought about that way: As my buddy.

You didn't want her as your enemy.

She'd say something like, "Okay! So you're a goody-goody!" and that would be the end of you, at least so far as I was concerned.

Or if she really didn't like you she'd just blow a really big bubblegum bubble while you were trying to talk to her and you'd know she wasn't paying you any serious attention.

I'd climbed the tree because it was there. And I could do that. It was free. I was free. I wanted to test myself: How high could I climb?

And I wanted to smother myself with apples: Smelling them and inspecting them up close and counting them and wondering about worms and just nestling next to apples in an apple tree.

I felt so clean! I felt so safe!

I felt myself far away from Valerie and her beautiful, tall boyfriend, Jeffrey Underwood, when the cops busted up his face and kicked out his teeth because they were cops and they were white people and Jeffrey lived on our block and he hadn't done anything besides that besides live on our block because he belonged there on our block and then the cops chased him to the roof and they caught him and they messed everything up and nothing was the same after that: Nothing.

I felt myself far far far away from my father who had started calling me "a whore" and I didn't know "a whore" from an owl but I found out what he meant and I thought my father was crazy as a matter of fact but what could I do about that when I called the police one time to report my father because he kept beating me and the policeman told me I should "try to be a good girl" and now my father was calling me "a whore" because for Halloween I put some of my mother's lipstick on my lips as part of my costume and I am nine years old and how can I be selling my body with my mother's lipstick on it?

⁂

But then the Robin Hood Camp grown-ups got so upset about my staying up in the apple tree that I had no idea what to do because now my honor seemed to be at stake.

The whole point of the apple tree was that I was free but if I came down because grown-ups more or less told me I had to or I should then I wouldn't be free anymore and I'd be out of the apple tree and just standing on the ground and so it was a problem and I didn't know how to solve it in a way that would feel all right and be all right and then the camp director sent for my parents!

I couldn't believe it!

She called my parents! My parents came all the way from Brooklyn to get me out of an apple tree.

When I saw them I felt so ashamed. I knew they'd had to travel so long and take off from work and this white lady had called to tell them I was being bad and I did not feel good about that either.

But they stood there under the apple tree, looking up at me.

And I didn't know if they weren't saying anything because I was hung up in the apple tree or because they were surrounded by white people and so they didn't want to say anything real anyway but that made me feel ashamed and still I couldn't see how or why I could come down and then Jodi showed up and she was chewing and cracking her gum real hard and she just gestured with her head that I should climb and then jump down and then follow her because there were better things we had to do more or less immediately so I climbed and I jumped down and I hugged my mother and I hugged my father and then Jodi and I raced each other to softball practice.

After this, some of the counselors decided Jodi was "a bad influence" on me.

She wore a rabbit's foot.

She never washed it.

She didn't read books.

She read magazines.

Together we kept getting into trouble, like setting loose the rowboats after lights out.

They assumed Jodi was "wrong" while I was "young and impressionable."

And one night in the rec hall, this counselor we called Miss Phyl stood in front of Jodi's face and told Jodi to take off that "stupid, filthy rabbit's foot" and I could see Jodi was stunned. Jodi was hurt. And I truly hated Miss Phyl. And I truly loved Jodi.

I truly did.

And not then, but the next summer, we became a secret society, the Daredevils, and we each cut our wrists and mixed our blood so we became blood brothers, and it's true that Jodi had more brainstorms than anybody else about ways to prove you were not a coward: That was true.

That's why I loved her.

And not then, but the next summer, we made the playoffs for a softball championship and the game was starting in fifteen minutes and no one could find Jodi and she hadn't shown up and I went looking for her and I found her reading a movie magazine because she said she didn't feel like playing but I was positive we'd lose without Jodi and before then we'd stuck by each other thick so there never was a question about thin and this game was for the championship and anyway I didn't want to play if Jodi wasn't going to so I begged her to change her mind and we had only ten minutes left and I hit her I slapped her hard and my hand burned the air between us and she stared at me and I just looked back at her because it just felt too late to say anything but she said okay she'd play so she played which is the only reason why we won that game that game and I wanted to burn my hand for hours afterward I wanted to burn it burn it up.

But Jodi laughed and said, "What's the big deal? You lost your temper but we won the game! Didn't we?!"

That next summer was also when the hated pushy counselor, Miss Phyl, loaned me *The Razor's Edge* and *Tender Is the Night* and *Time Must Have a Stop* and *The Magic Mountain*.

I read the first two.

I hadn't known about books like these before. Bunches of words talked about the feelings of strange men and strange women I had big trouble trying to understand.

They acted like no one I'd ever met. But still I could read about all their fears, all their real wishes, plain as plain, page after page.

It was peculiar.

Now I knew people could be really different from me, inside.

And I liked finding out about that.

⁂

This pretty lady was lying on top of me. I wasn't sure if nineteen was her age or the size of her waist but there was no doubt about how very pretty she was lying on top of me and telling me silly stuff into my ear and nobody ever lay on top of me before that or beside me before that but here was Pretty Miss Kitty on top of me and she felt long and wide and close and hot and not too heavy for me underneath her I didn't think and I liked it but also I was not breathing so well because I was so excited because why was she doing that with my bunkmates just inches away from her and me and what if somebody woke up and found us like that?

I just wished she would tiptoe out of the cabin because I was about to die from excitement and terror and why was she doing this? Why?

And now her soft mouth kissed my cheeks and I felt like I needed to pass out because that kiss felt so soft to me I couldn't think anymore because that kiss made me want the feeling of her soft mouth on my face forever.

I was ten years old.

❧ ❧ ❧

Pretty Miss Kitty was dark-skinned like my Uncle Teddy: Dark chocolate like you could just about drink it thick and smooth and sweet and not quite steaming from a cup you'd want to hold and smell and stare at and nobody bother you about that. I followed her around.

❧ ❧ ❧

She was the new music counselor and she played the piano and she never once looked at the keys; any song and she could play it right away and never need to learn the notes!

She played our raggedy old piano in the rec hall.

We'd be sitting on the floor and I'd be noticing the scratched-up surface of the piano and the wobbling of the piano bench and then she'd run her fingers up and down that corny, yellow-stained keyboard and then just like everybody else I was only listening to the music. I was only listening to the music that she made.

❧ ❧ ❧

Pretty Miss Kitty was an American Negro. She came from "down South."

More than anything else she wanted to be a singer.

She was studying music at Fisk University.

That was "down South": Memphis, Tennessee.

Her family lived somewhere in South Carolina.

And I'd try to trick Pretty Miss Kitty into saying "Carolina" any way I could.

Anything she said would make me laugh, make me happy, because she always had this Southern accent that changed every word into something new and funny and hard to hear, except my name.

She called me Ju-nie.

I heard that.

* * *

All the other counselors were white. I was very proud of Pretty Miss Kitty.

She talked to me.

She told me how down South was not the same as Robin Hood or Brooklyn or anything I knew.

White people hated everybody.

You had to step off the sidewalk for white people walking your way.

Sometimes they burned down your house.

They would choose a big oak tree in the Negro part of town and then they'd hang a man, a Negro man.

They'd hang him from the tree.
They'd leave him hanging there.
Nobody could take him down
or they'd come back for you.
They came back at night.
Nobody could do anything about them.

⁂

I would just look at her.

⁂

Miss Kitty asked me what I wanted to be when I grew up.

No one had ever asked me that before. I said I wanted to be a great man. I wanted to be a great writer.

I was going to be a poet.

I was going to take care of her.

I would make things change down South.

⁂

Who were these white people around me?

Why were they different from down South?

What did it mean, "the difference is only skin deep"?

And what about Jodi and my other blood brothers?

And what about Kenny "the kitchen boy" I had a crush on?

⁂

The night after Pretty Miss Kitty lay down on top of me was our last night of the summer.

Somehow they'd built a campfire on a raft and floated that on the lake.

We shivered in the darkness by the water.

Counselors were crying.

Some of the campers were crying.

Jodi and I exchanged glances but we didn't laugh or cry.

I could feel sadness around me. But I didn't feel sad.

I thought I should pay attention.

I thought I shouldn't show any disrespect.

Maybe when I got to be a grown-up I'd feel sad about a last day, too.

And at that time I wouldn't want some silly kid laughing at me.

⁂

So we sat there and we sang songs and held hands in silence.

And then Pretty Miss Kitty lifted her voice into a solo singing of a song that was better than church.

She was way out on the dark lake beyond the fire.

You couldn't see the rowboat holding her above the water.

"... For all we know
this may end as just a dream
we come and go
like the ripples of a stream..."

And her voice was like a soft mouth kissing the darkness itself.

And I prayed that nothing would ever stop that song.

She was singing
her song
and everybody could hear it.
And she was singing
and singing
her song
for me.

part eleven

THE ONLY LAST CHAPTER OF MY CHILDHOOD

All of a sudden we were baseball fans. We were rooting for the Brooklyn Dodgers. We were filling up the bleacher seats at Ebbets Field.

This was better than Joe Louis, because you could see Jackie Robinson.

You could buy a ticket and see him. And every time he ran from the dugout we'd just scream, "Jackie! Jackie!"

That was the chant: "Jackie! Jackie! Jackie!"

He was very handsome.

He had graduated from college.

He was married to an educated Negro lady.

He was the first Negro baseball player to make the major leagues.

He was the "only" one.

He could slide into first base faster than the pitcher could throw the ball.

And he could hit.

⁂

I got pretty interested in baseball. My parents acted like the Dodgers were going to save the world.

They'd hired Jackie, hadn't they?

And Jackie could play, couldn't he?

Nothing was impossible anymore.

And if Jackie ever hit a home run then the shouts and pounding feet could wake the dead.

※※※

But I was wondering why Jackie Robinson had to be "the first"; why he had to hope to become a *first*?

I was wondering why anyone had to be so good, so fast or smart, just to become the first and the only Negro.

This *first* thing got on my nerves.

※※※

From our house it was always a long bus ride to a good supermarket or fruit stand or library or post office. And now there was going to be a long bus ride to school for me every day.

Because I got straight *A*s, my father was able to enroll me at Midwood High. It was supposed to be the best.

It was more than an hour's ride away, each way.

And when I got there, I was the only colored girl, or boy, waiting for the bell.

There were fifteen hundred students standing outside that school, and I was the "only" one.

I didn't like it.

I felt small.

I felt outnumbered.

I was surrounded by "them."

And there was no "we."

There was only me.

I didn't like it.

And because I'd been skipped two years ahead, I was like a pint-sized mascot to my class: I was twelve years old and a sophomore, and the whole thing felt wrong.

⁂

The ride was just too long!

I'd fall asleep on the bus.

But when it got to be winter I couldn't sleep. It was too cold.

I sat wide awake, snuggling my books inside my arms.

Then one morning this boy got on the bus.

He sat across from me, so I couldn't really look at him.

But I could tell he was cute.

I could feel it.

He was cute.

⁂

After I first laid eyes on Herbie Wilson, Jr., *first* took on new meanings for me. It had nothing to do with white people.

For the first time, I tried to look nice for school.

I brushed my hair as carefully as I brushed my shoes.

I double-checked my braids to make sure they weren't coming apart.

I experimented with the stacking of my books so I wouldn't always be dropping them, or anything else embarrassing.

I tried to hide the Kleenex my mother made me carry everywhere.

I wanted to be pretty.

I could tell he was too old for me so I wanted to grow up.

He was the first perfect boy I had ever seen.

⁂

He was sixteen.

⁂

I didn't know his name.

But I knew he lived in a nicer neighborhood than mine; that's where he got on the bus.

And I knew he went to Tilden High; that's where he got off the bus.

And I knew I didn't care about anything besides seeing him again.

⁂

My father was determined I'd be gone, "out of the streets," by next September.

He asked Father Coleman to recommend a strict Christian prep school for girls.

Father Coleman did not hesitate:

He'd write a letter to the Northfield Schools at once.

He said they'd been founded by "an evangelist," Dwight L. Moody, in 1881, and now, Northfield boasted the highest academic standing.

My father said it was a "finishing" school: I'd learn table manners, table conversation, grooming, and ladylike posture.

Northfield sounded very far away to me.

⁂

I wanted—I needed—somebody to introduce us.

But everybody just laughed at me.

He couldn't be that cute!

⁂

My mother didn't argue anymore.

And, anyway, my father didn't need her
to agree.

⁂

One minute I was thinking about the beautiful shape of his head and the next minute he was asking me to dance.

He was there.

He had come to the Halloween party at St. Phillip's.

He stood in front of me, smiling.

I gave him my hand.

⁂

Because Northfield insisted on an interview, my father had to take three days off from work.

He was completely dressed up.

And we traveled for most of a day just getting there.

In the morning I got a good look at what they called "the campus."

Altogether there were ten thousand acres belonging to the school.

It was clear to me that we had landed on another planet.

⁂

Valerie was irate!

Herbie Wilson, Jr., *was,* in fact, *that cute!*

Why would he bother about a stupid
kid like me?

⁂

This white lady was showing us around
the school.

This was a dorm.

That was a dorm.

This was a classroom building.

That was the science laboratory.

That was the auditorium.

This was the soccer field.

Those were the tennis courts.

That was one of the swimming pools.

That was the pond for ice-skating or ice hockey.

These were the vineyards.

Those were the cows.

This was the chapel.

That was the ski jump.

This was the path to the bookstore.

And she wondered if we might have any questions.

⁂

For the first time, I couldn't think of anything to say.

He'd hold my hand and we'd walk like that and he'd keep asking me about so many things but I just couldn't stop giggling because I loved him.

He loved me!

And I loved the leather jacket that he wore; it was light brown like his eyes.

And I loved how his long legs seemed unpredictable and quick to the left or to the right.

I loved how he was almost too skinny.

I loved the delicate look and feel of his muscular hand.

I loved the stray hairs growing above his upper lip.

I loved how he hugged me close and my face nuzzled well below his shoulders.

I loved how he didn't mind what other people said about me being so young and so silly.

I loved how he made me feel I didn't
have to do anything at all.

Or almost nothing: He was pretty set on teaching me to "French Kiss." But that didn't sound like a great idea to me. And he got Valerie to take me to some movie so, anyway, I'd learn how. But then he stopped talking about it. And that was when he changed my mind.

He said I was his sweetheart.

And I was.

* * *

I was left alone with pencils and an exam.

This was the I.Q. test segment of the interview.

It was so quiet and sunny!

I tried to remember other tests like this one.

Why was the room always so
comfortable and dreamy?

⁂

I forgot about my parents.

When Herbie Wilson, Jr., took my hand I lost track of a regular life.

I went off guard.

And the last thing I wanted was a fight.

So it was just lucky that they liked him: They thought he was "clean-cut" and his folks seemed to them "very respectable."

Mr. and Mrs. Wilson teased me a lot about being "so smart for such a little girl." But it never felt mean.

They had decided to join our church, and Herbie Wilson, Jr., would soon become an acolyte.

⁂

Suddenly there were four white people talking to me and my father.

My "I.Q." really surprised them.

They wanted me at Northfield!

Why wait until September?

Couldn't I come in January?

They'd give me a full scholarship.

They'd take care of what they called "incidentals."

They'd pay for my transportation!

Why wait?

I didn't say anything because I knew this was not up to me.

My father seemed bewildered by all the excitement. But then he remembered my mother. He told them he'd have to talk with her.

I just sat listening to all of this.

And then the white lady from that morning peered at me: "Well! But let's hear from June! Would you like to come to Northfield?"

I knew if I said, "No, thank you," my father would kill me. So I said I couldn't really tell what it would be like to live so far away from home.

"Oh!," she said.

I could see my father lowering his head into his neck. So I asked if school might be, sort of, exactly like summer camp.

And she said, "Yes!"

So I didn't listen anymore; I already knew it wouldn't be the same!

At Northfield, you had to go to chapel six times a week. And there were "House Prayers" twice a day with your dorm-mates, besides.

That white lady had said so. I wasn't listening to her any-more.

But the white man sitting next to her took over:

"So! It's all settled! She's coming in September!"

And he stood up. And everyone stood up.

And he offered to shake my hand.

I was glad I knew how to do that part of it.

I lifted my head and looked him in the eye.

I shook his hand.

And I wondered if I was about to become a *first.*

⁂ ⁂ ⁂

Church and Herbie Wilson, Jr.?!

I was standing in the choir loft but I could hardly stand still.

He was the one carrying the cross all the way up the aisle.

Around me the organ pipes shook or trembled with a melody as familiar to me as his hair, his lips.

It seemed so obvious that he should be the one.

"Oh, Lamb of God
Oh, Lamb of God. . . "

He was almost smiling.

⁂ ⁂ ⁂

I actually liked the idea of "Bible Studies" and daily chapel and prayers around the clock! I just didn't see what any of that had to do with Robin Hood.

⁂

He'd come to the house and he'd sit close beside me on the parlor couch and he'd put his arm around me and sometimes we'd just stay like that or sometimes we'd start laughing and we couldn't stop laughing or sometimes he'd tell me about baseball practice and how he wanted to be the first Negro pitcher in the major leagues and how the coach said he had "a fair chance" at making it and sometimes he'd tell me about the Boy Scouts because he was a Boy Scout Leader and sometimes he'd wear his uniform and come over like that with the Boy Scout bandana knotted around his neck and he gave me his high school senior ring and he gave me my first Valentine card and my first Valentine present a Valentine bracelet and he would just kiss me on the mouth and he would just kiss me and kiss me and then we'd start laughing again and sometimes I would feel I would think that maybe I should just die right then before something bad could happen to Herbie Wilson, Jr., or to me.

⁂

I was worn out from the interview. But it was my father who slept most of the way back home.

⁂

Herbie Wilson, Jr., was taking me to see my first Broadway play, *Member of the Wedding*.

I was going on my first real date!

I was wearing my rose-colored taffeta dress and my mother had washed and twisted my hair into long curls and I had my gloves and pocketbook to match and I was trying out my brand-new black suede shoes with an ankle strap and I asked my mother how do I look? How do I look?

But she shook her head:
"Don't be worrying about that.
Any boy interested to see you won't
be caring about how you look!"
I stared at my mother.
"It's not looks that you have!
It's a brain!"
I couldn't catch my breath.
I didn't believe her!
I didn't believe her!

And then there was Herbie Wilson, Jr., ringing the bell. And I went to the gate to open it and he was wearing a tie and a new suit and the old lace-up shoes he always liked to wear and we went to the city and we watched this play about a white girl with her Negro "Mammy" looking after her and at one point the girl uses this huge knife to slice at something on her foot and that made the biggest impression on me about *Member of the Wedding* except for afterward when Herbie Wilson, Jr., took me to the Times Square Crossroads Café and we sat at this tiny table with a blue-and-white-checkered tablecloth and he ordered strawberry shortcake for both of us and a bottle of beer for himself and a glass of milk for me and I felt pretty sure I must look all right.

⁂

I wasn't too happy about maybe having to choose
between having brains and being pretty.
I wasn't too happy that maybe somebody else
had already made that choice for me.

⁂

I had to tell him they were sending me away.
But he was leaving, too.
He'd enter Howard University in the fall.
Maybe we should break up before he left.
He wanted to feel free to see older women; maybe
even a woman his own age.
He would never stop loving me.
I knew that was true.
And I didn't care.

I was losing my first love.

I was losing my only first love.

I knew that was true.

⁂

My mother didn't see me off.

My father brought me to the railroad station by himself.

Just outside Track 22, we faced each other:

"Okay! Little Soldier! G'wan! G'wan!

You gwine make me proud!"

And I could hear nothing else

And I wondered who would meet my train.